LIVINGSTONE'S LONDON

A Celebration of People and Places

LIVINGSTONE'S LONDON

A Celebration of People and Places

Ken Livingstone

MUSWELL
PRESS

First published by Muswell Press in 2019

Typeset by M Rules
Copyright © Ken Livingstone

Ken Livingstone asserts the moral right
to be identified as the author of this work.

Printed and bound by CPI Group (UK) Ltd, Croydon CR0 4YY.

This book is a work of fiction and, except in the case of historical fact, any
resemblence to actual persons, living or dead, is purely coincidental.

A CIP catalogue record for this book
is available from the British Library

ISBN 9781999613570

Muswell Press
London
N6 5HQ
www.muswell-press.co.uk

Thank you Emma for all your help.
I hope that London will give Mia and Tom
a life as good as it gave me.

CONTENTS

CHAPTER ONE

Early Days

In 2018, for the second year running, London was named the most dynamic city in Europe in a study of 130 major cities. We topped the rankings in innovation, inspiration, interconnection, investment and infrastructure, and came third in inclusion.

To have been born in 1945 and brought up in London in the decades after the Second World War was amazing. Each year everything got better. My generation of Londoners is undoubtedly the luckiest in history; even as kids we knew that we were living in the greatest city on earth, at the heart of the greatest empire in human history. My parents' generation grew up in a world where many still believed Jesus had come to Britain before his death, which inspired William Blake's famous line: 'And did those feet in ancient time/ Walk upon England's mountains green', from his poem 'Jerusalem'. Some also believed that Joseph Arimathea, who buried Jesus in his family tomb, had brought part of the crown of thorns worn by Jesus to England and built a church at Glastonbury.

The British dream of continuing to be a superpower after the war was boosted when a British expedition was the first to conquer Mount Everest and the news was held back to coincide with the day of the Queen's coronation in June 1953, prompting the *Daily Express* headline 'All This And Everest Too'. The following year saw a similar reinforcement to our national pride when Roger Bannister became the first man to run a mile in just three minutes and fifty-nine seconds, which triggered more celebration in the papers: 'So Britain has been the first to conquer Everest and achieve the four-minute mile.' Another paper proudly boasted: 'Britain has pioneered the way. So let us have no more talk of an effete and worn-out nation.'

Growing up while our parents discussed our triumph over the greatest evil in human history meant that we felt safe and secure. But we didn't know that in the decades to come, everything was going to keep improving as we watched London being transformed from the horrors of the damage done by wartime bombing.

I was lucky to be born and brought up for the first five years of my life off Streatham High Road, which was one of the busiest shopping centres in south London. It had the amazing Pratts department store, which Mum and Nan would wander around with me daydreaming about being able to buy some of the stuff on display. Occasionally Mum would go into a bright red phone box on the street in order to place bets on that day's horse racing. We only got a phone in our home when I was twelve.

Although the bombing in Streatham hadn't been anything like as bad as in the East End of London, over 4,000 Lambeth homes had been destroyed and 38,000 damaged. In the early 1950s my friends and I would spend most of our time playing on the old bomb sites. One of the problems was rats and mice. Their population soared in the aftermath of the bombing, and Lambeth council had to employ rat catchers to try and contain the problem, but as late as 1962 the council was getting over 1,000 complaints a year.

Looking back, London didn't just go through reconstruction but presided over an amazing and dynamic cultural change in almost every aspect of our lives. The concentration of theatres, cinemas, sports stadia, museums and galleries meant that we had so much to do. Post war London had fifty-five major theatres (compared to just thirty-nine in Paris) and 184 museums (New York had just 101). Even more dramatic was our lead in music venues. London had 400 to just 122 in Paris. We also had 3,117 bars compared to 1,800 in New York. Across the city we staged over 200 festivals a year, compared to forty in Paris. There was so much we could in London without crossing continents. I can remember my parents coming back from watching the stage versions of the musical *Oklahoma!*, Arthur Miller's *Death of a Salesman,* and Ivor Novello's *King's Rhapsody*, but perhaps the most amazing was *A Streetcar Named Desire* with Vivien Leigh and Laurence Olivier, although Mum and Dad didn't see it immediately, as people were queuing for twenty-four hours in order to get in. Tickets were much cheaper then and a working-class couple could afford to go to a West End theatre.

Of course, they didn't take me to the theatre, but two or three times a week we went to the cinema to see such amazing films as *Doctor in the House*, for which there were queues all over London waiting for the next showing. The films I loved were mainly sci-fi, but *The Dam Busters* was clearly the most-watched film of that era. When eventually I had children, we went to see all the *Star Wars* films. National figures showed that most families were going to the cinema at least twice a week in the late 1940s, and that would only change after commercial television came along in 1955. Even more exciting, I would be taken to the zoo every time some amazing new animal appeared. Back in 1947 it was Guy the Gorilla and eleven years later Chi Chi the giant panda. I also remember the long queue as we all waited to see the first ever polar bear cub born in captivity.

The most wonderful experience of that time was when my dad took me to see the Planetarium, which had just opened in Baker Street in 1958. After a few minutes watching the depiction of the stars circling over our heads inside the great dome, the presenter announced this is what the sky would look like if we had no atmosphere, and the audience gasped as suddenly we saw 9,000 stars above our heads. The most significant impact of the Planetarium was it gave you an understanding of the scale of our universe and how small our little planet was in comparison to all of this. I was so angry when Madame Tussauds closed the Planetarium, because all our kids should have gone and seen it.

Back in those days I was gripped by science fiction, particularly the books of Arthur C. Clarke, such as *The City and the Stars* and *Reach for Tomorrow*. He also did brilliant non-fiction, such as *Profiles of the Future*. One of the main themes of science fiction in those days was that humans would spread out not just through our solar system but to colonise the whole galaxy, just as 500 years ago the Spanish, French and English spread out to colonise the whole world. All this suddenly seemed possible when there came an amazing announcement on 4 October 1957 that Russia had launched the first satellite into space, called Sputnik and no bigger than a beach ball. Then, just a few weeks later, the Russian dog Laika circled the world in Sputnik 2.

The impact on the USA, as they realised Russia was over-taking them in the space race, was made even worse when the Americans broadcast live the launch of their Vanguard Missile. The world watched as after rising just two feet it crashed back and the press called it Flopnik. The Americans finally launched their first satellite the next month. But there wasn't just the space race – there was also the nuclear arms race, with Russia and America exploding bigger and bigger hydrogen bombs, with the radioactive fallout spreading around the planet, Eventually, public concern that that radioactive fallout was getting into our bodies led the super-powers to start testing their bombs underground.

By the time the Americans finally landed on the moon in 1969 it seemed inevitable that we were going to spread out across our galaxy. President Nixon claimed there would be Americans on Mars by 1980 and the media was filled with stories about how we would be mining the asteroids and landing on the moons of Jupiter and Saturn well before the end of the twentieth century; then we would begin our first flights to other stars.

So why didn't all this happen? There are three basic reasons. One is that it is hugely more expensive than people thought it would be. America's moon programme cost them £76 billion (in today's money). Secondly, we also now know the levels of radiation in deep space would be absolutely lethal for long-term travelling and finally, we need to remember that everything about our bodies has evolved based on living on this planet. When astronauts return to earth after spending just half a year circling the earth in a satellite, they have to be carried out of their spacecraft because they have lost the ability to walk after spending six months without gravity. But as I walked out of the Planetarium, I was certain my dream of being an astronaut would one day come true. Very disappointing.

Perhaps the biggest difference between London then and now was the lack of racial diversity. There were small non-white communities, mainly in the East End or around Soho, but it was only in 1948 that the Windrush generation of Caribbeans arrived (just 492 Jamaicans) and were housed initially in wartime shelters in Clapham. I had been born in the Tory suburb of Streatham and one of my earliest memories is my nan excitedly pointing across the road, saying, 'Look, there's a black man.' Even though my secondary school was just south of Brixton, there were no black children because the first wave of immigrants left their children at home and the only time I talked to a black person was when buying a ticket from the bus conductor. It was only when I started work in 1962, and there were three technicians from Ghana working in the cancer-research unit, that I started having proper friendships with people of other races. If you want to get a full view of what the world was like in those days, you should read Andrea Levy's brilliant book *Small Island*, which won two awards for the best book of 2005.

We were a short bus ride from the Festival of Britain, which opened on the South Bank in 1951 on the 100th anniversary of the Great Exhibition of 1851. Up until then we had clapped-out old trams, but they were being replaced by buses all over London. The last tram went in 1952. Luckily I was six when the festival opened, because for some bizarre reason they had decided that no child under five should be allowed in, so my poor sister Linda was left at home with my nan. When we arrived at the festival I was amazed at the size of the Dome of Discovery (the largest dome in the world, 365 feet in diameter, one for each day of the year) and the 296-foot-tall Skylon. Sadly, I wasn't old enough to be terribly impressed with the sculptures by Henry Moore, Jacob Epstein and Barbara Hepworth. But even better than the Festival of Britain, and at the same time, the Battersea Park funfair opened. I was really annoyed when my parents didn't let me go in the giant spinning rota drum, as they were frightened I might end up breaking a bone. Although the funfair stayed open for decades, the new Tory government under Churchill decided to close the festival after accusing Herbert Morrison, then Labour's deputy prime minister, of having wasted too much money on it.

One of the best things about growing up in London was that there were so many parks. My first five years in Streatham were in a tiny little flat without a bathroom, but in those days councils ran communal baths and laundries (back in 1950 only 46 per cent of homes in Britain had their own bathroom, and even as late as 1971 in inner London 37 per cent of families shared a bathroom, with 21 per cent of families still sharing a home). Although our flat was very cramped, we were a short walk from Streatham Common, where on sunny days Nan and Mum would take me so I could run around with Linda in the lovely little woodlands.

When we moved to our new flat on the Tulse Hill Estate, it had its own bathroom and, even more amazingly, a bedroom each for both me and my sister. We were so excited with this new home that Mum and Dad talked about staying there until they died. Once again we were just down the road from Brockwell Park, another wonderful place to explore and play in, and with a lido that Dad would take us to on hot days. But seven years later Mum and Dad got caught up in the rush of people planning to buy their own home, even though they had to struggle to get the £400 deposit. When they bought their home in West Norwood in 1957 we were still near a park – Norwood Park.

,Wherever we lived when I was growing up, there was always a library where we could go and choose from a huge range of books. Back in those days hardback books were expensive and it would be two years before you could get a paperback version, so there was always a long waiting list at the library for people anxious to read another James Bond book. When I got older I used the library to read magazines I couldn't afford to buy, like *The Economist*.

Of course, the most significant event of those years was the Queen's coronation on 2 June 1953. Luckily my mum's best friend had just bought a television, so we got the bus over to their house to watch it. There was no one else on the bus and there was virtually nobody out on the street, as everyone was already sitting around their radios or joining in the crowds to watch the Queen being driven by. It was breathtaking to sit there for the first time looking at a dense wooden box with a tiny concave screen not much bigger than a square foot and grainy black-and-white pictures. But for a seven-year-old the lengthy ceremony soon got quite boring.

Twelve years later I was totally gripped watching the live broadcast of Winston Churchill's funeral. In the days before his burial 320,000 people had filed past his coffin in Westminster Hall. The life of Churchill dominated the news in the days following his death, which unleashed enormous emotion, particularly for my parents' generation, who saw him as the man who saved his nation, and they were right to believe that.

We now know the real history of that period. When the Tory prime minister, Neville Chamberlain, was forced to resign in 1940, the bulk of Tory MPs feared the war would end in disaster and possible defeat, so they wanted to do some deal with Hitler. The person most likely to do that was the only other potential prime minister, Lord Halifax. Fortunately, as Halifax was in the House of Lords, that undermined his chances, and Churchill was more determined to win the job. Churchill had stood out on the Tory benches for years as the strongest opponent of the Nazis and was prepared to pay whatever price it took in order to defeat them. When he became prime minster, with support from the Labour benches, he created a coalition that included Labour. Just a few days later France fell, and for the following year Britain stood alone in the world in resisting the tide of Nazism. My parents always complained that it took a long time for the Americans to come in on our side.

While Churchill was an absolutely brilliant prime minister in preserving democracy and defeating the greatest evil of our times, he had been deeply reactionary as Chancellor of the Exchequer in the 1920s by returning us to the gold standard, which meant an overvalued pound, hitting our export market. He was also totally opposed to allowing independence to India and other colonies. But all that is overshadowed by his influence in creating the post-war world based on democracy and freedom.

Weather in the 1940s was so different from now. Back in 1947 the Thames was frozen at Windsor and there was 17° of frost (-9°C/15°F). Our energy supplies struggled and we occasionally had fuel shutdowns for three hours in the morning, between nine and twelve, and two hours in the afternoon, between two and four. It wasn't just that our weather was quite miserable in those days – sometimes it was lethal. Every home had a coal fire and most of our industries used coal. My first domestic job of the day was to get up in the morning and clear out all the old ashes and then light a new fire. Every spring Mum had to take down all the curtains to wash them because they were filled with coal dust; the washing water became black. This was before we had a washing machine, so all laundry was done by hand and all year round we hung up the clothes indoors to dry them.

The worst consequence of everybody using coal fires came in 1952 with the Great Smog, in which over 3,500

Londoners died and my sister and I weren't allowed out of the house for days, even though this meant missing school. I sat by the window but couldn't see the other side of the road. Why on earth did the London City Council (LCC) build our flats in Irby House with coal fires rather than electric? In 1956 the government passed the Clean Air Act, which began the dramatic reduction in the use of coal and opened the way for a wave of central heating.

It wasn't just the air that was bad; in 1953 a flood on the Thames Estuary swamped 24,000 homes and killed 300 people. It would take nearly twenty years before the Greater London Council (the GLC, which replaced the LCC) decided to build the Thames Barrier, which wasn't completed until 1982, meaning we lived through those decades with the risk of a catastrophic flood in central London. When I became the leader of the GLC in 1981, one of my biggest worries was that a flood would come before the barrier was finished. Fortunately, it was completed just in time and raised twice during 1982. Now it is raised many more times each year. Part of the problem is that at high tide today the Thames is three metres higher than in Roman times, as the London clay sinks deeper and the ice caps melt, so by the middle of this century we will need a bigger barrier and governments have to start working on it now. When I was London Mayor I failed to get the government to focus on this because most politicians are only concerned about the next election, not what's going to happen in half a century.

As the government tried to tackle Britain's vast wartime debt it even had to increase rationing to cover bread, and life did seem rather tough. A Gallup poll showed that 42 per cent of us wanted to emigrate, which was up from just 19 per cent two years earlier. It was only in 1948 that for the first time a black teacher was given a job in a London school. His name was Eustace Braithwaite and was depicted as the teacher forming close bonds with his students and fighting adversity in the 1967 film *To Sir With Love*.

The conservative mood of the times was reflected when the *Manchester Guardian* newspaper (which changed its name to the *Guardian* in 1959) warned that the state welfare system would see an 'increase of congenitally deformed and feckless people', and Bernard Griffin, Archbishop of Westminster, persuaded the government not to bring Catholic hospitals into the NHS. The BBC was just as bad, banning any jokes about lavatories, effeminacy in men and immorality of any kind, including suggestive references to chambermaids, prostitution, ladies' underwear and honeymoon couples. Later on, the *Carry On* films would become a huge success as they exaggerated all these ridiculous bans.

Although 75 per cent of Brits were working class, the number of working-class Labour MPs had slipped from 72 per cent in 1935 to just 38 per cent in 1945. While the weather was not good, a lot else was beginning to change, with newfangled products like washing machines, vacuum cleaners and fridges, the appearance of Nescafé instant coffee, which became my favourite drink, and suddenly you could buy frozen chicken pies and fish fingers. The first launderette opened in May 1949 in Bayswater and by 1955 a majority of homes had a vacuum cleaner, one in five a washing machine, and one in ten a fridge.

Crime was so low that most people left their front door unlocked for a large part of the day and people didn't feel the need to chain their bikes up. It was only in 1957 that for the first time that motorbikes were made with locks. In that year the police recorded half a million crimes a year, compared to 4.5 million forty years later. Eleven thousand were violent crimes in 1957, and forty years later that had risen to a quarter of a million.

CHAPTER TWO

School Days

Although you might think I had no worries about my life, I had nearly died from gastroenteritis just before I was three. It meant I grew up as the smallest boy in my class and it was only when I got into my early twenties that I caught up with everybody else.

A major change in education policy was the government's decision that kids would no longer leave school at the age of fourteen and this meant a massive new school building programme and the arrival of comprehensive schools replacing secondary moderns. London's first new comprehensive school at Blackheath had 1,700 children when it opened in 1954.

Two years later, when I started my secondary school, I went to the brand new eight-story Tulse Hill School, which, with 2,300 boys, was the largest school in Britain. It was disappointing to fail my eleven-plus, as three quarters of us did, but we just took it to be the norm. There were thirteen forms in each year and the top three were considered academic (I was in the sixth grade) but for the rest of us much of our time was spent in the twenty-six workshops, six gymnasiums, two floors of laboratories and one floor with art rooms. They had been built so the school could prepare us for apprenticeships in building and manufacturing when we left. Mr Thomas the headmaster, having come from being the deputy head of the prestigious Dulwich College, imposed a rigid class structure on our school. The top three academic forms were virtually all middle class and the bottom ones the poorest, working class. None of us expected to go to university in those days – only 4 per cent of kids did – but among the working classes it was just 1 per cent.

The worst thing about the school was the bullying. Fellow pupil John Land told my biographer Andrew Hoskin, 'They used to say that if you could survive Tulse Hill School, you could survive anywhere,' and another pupil, John Harris remembered 'older boys hanging a science teacher out of a window on the first floor by his braces'. As just about the smallest boy in the school, I worked out that the best way to avoid being bullied was to make people laugh. But if that didn't work, I had to stand up to the bullies, because if you don't it just gets worse.

At the end of my second year I was upgraded to the academic second tier, but this meant a complete change in my classmates. I went from a form of predominantly working-class kids to a form of middle class and I never really fitted in with them. By the time I got to my fourth year I started skipping classes and bunking off to play in the abandoned and slightly derelict windmill just a little way up the road in Brixton. This was the last windmill standing in London and had been neglected for years, but fortunately has now been restored by Lambeth Borough Council.

I had just turned twelve when Mum and Dad bought their first home. In order to pay off our mortgage, Dad had to get another job in the evenings, shifting scenery at Streatham Hill Theatre. This was the biggest theatre in Britain, and once a play finished its run in the West End it usually came to Streatham for a few weeks before moving on to its nationwide tour. Just before Christmas 1958 Dad told me he had got me a job there as well. The star of the Christmas pantomime was going to be the game-show host Hughie Green. This was the first famous person I had met, and I was so impressed by him but quite shocked when he told me that my job would be to pretend to be a member of the audience when he invited men and boys to come up on stage to see which of us could win a contest most quickly by being able to put on women's underwear over our trousers. As we all stood there holding knickers up, he asked each of us a question, which was 'Do you know what these are?' and I had to reply, 'I've seen them on the washing line.' I couldn't believe I was being paid £1 and ten shillings a week for just five minutes' work each night.

My admiration for Hughie Green evaporated in the mid-1970s when the news broke that he had secretly plotted to try and persuade the military to overthrow Harold Wilson's Labour government, as he believed Britain should be saved from socialism under Wilson. He also campaigned to undermine the trade embargo on the racist regime in

Rhodesia (now Zimbabwe). Bizarrely, he also decided to broadcast an episode of his *Opportunity Knocks* game show from a Polaris nuclear submarine and went on to broadcast another one from the deck of an aircraft carrier.

I was incredibly lucky to have as my first form master, Philip Hobsbaum, a bearded East End-born secular Jewish socialist who was a distant relative of the radical lefty Eric Hobsbawm..Philip started getting us to learn about politics and debating. Years later he came to see me when I was leader of the Greater London Council (GLC) and told me he'd always expected I'd become a journalist or go into advertising, not to become a politician. When in one of his lessons he decided to stage a mock general election, he told me I had to be the Liberal candidate. At the age of eleven I had no idea what the Liberals were, and when I asked Dad, he said just take a bit of Labour policy and a bit of Tory policy: that's what the Liberals do. My other most important teacher was Raymond Rivers, my biology teacher, who opened up my interest in reptiles and amphibians and made me fall in love with science, which led me to become an atheist at the age of twelve.

Raymond taught me the importance of finding the facts and truth, but he was never popular with the headmaster because he was an atheist. I had always assumed he was also a socialist, but when I met him forty years later at City Hall I couldn't believe it when he told me he had always been a Tory and loved Mrs Thatcher. The school also produced several interesting characters, including the actors Tim Roth and Kenneth Cranham, the Jamaican-born poet

Linton Kwesi Johnson and the former *Guardian* journalist David Hencke.

Perhaps the most significant post-war change was the fact that there was no unemployment. I didn't get enough O Levels to get into the sixth form to study for A Levels, but when I left school in 1962 every boy got a job and I didn't meet an unemployed person until the mid-1970s. Politicians of both main parties had learned the lessons of the Great Depression of the 1930s and set out to create a Keynesian economy based on full employment by creating new jobs, increasing wages and fuelled by the highest levels of public and private investment in our history. In 1973 we achieved our best level ever, with 20 per cent of our economy's GDP going into investment. West Germany was doing even better in rebuilding their economy, by achieving 25 per cent. Because the Conservatives continued with the 1945 Attlee government's economic policies, our economy continued to grow and in 1959 the Tory prime minster Harold McMillan won the election with the slogan 'You've never had it so good', which was also true.

It wasn't just that we all got a job – after a few years many of us could afford to get a mortgage, or if we didn't earn enough we could get a council flat, because both Labour and Conservative governments and councils were building between 150,000 and 200,000 council homes a year.

Our family didn't get a television until 1955, so every evening we sat around listening to the radio and I was so transfixed by the science-fiction programme *Journey Into Space* that I dreamed of becoming an astronaut (called a spaceman in those days). Mum and Dad only got a telly when ITV started. Its first programme was to broadcast the boring speeches at the opening of a Guildhall dinner celebrating the launch of ITV, so we had wait until eight o'clock before real programmes started. That week we all became devoted to *I Love Lucy* and *Dragnet*, both from America. We also loved *Robin Hood* and the quiz shows *Take Your Pick* and *Double Your Money* with Hughie Green (with the top prize of £1,024). The high point of the week was *Sunday Night at the London Palladium* with Gracie Fields starring in the opening programme, but it was the comedian Tommy Trinder who was most popular, making us all laugh.

Although the BBC was always deferential when interviewing politicians, Robin Day's tough interviews on ITV changed all that. But the BBC did get something right in December 1954 when they televised George Orwell's *Nineteen Eighty-Four*. This unleashed a wave of press criticism, with MPs warning it had frightened some viewers because of its scary scenes. There was similar opposition to horror comics being imported from America. The National Union of Teachers campaigned to ban them for 'degrading the minds of young people'. At a cabinet meeting copies were passed round to ministers, who then pushed a law through Parliament that made them illegal. Mum and Dad never let me see one, but fortunately a new comic had come out in 1949 called *The Eagle*, which sold 900,000 copies a week, with its most memorable stories being the space adventures of Dan Dare.

We were still going to the cinema, though not as often, with some of the best films being about the Second World War. That Christmas Mum and Dad gave me the *Guinness*

Book of Records, which was the bestselling non-fiction book at the time, because it was used all over Britain in pub quizzes, and I spent days just browsing through the amazing lists of just about everything.

As my parents listened to the news, one of the main things they argued about was hanging. I was only eight when Derek Bentley was hanged in 1953 and this was perhaps the most controversial hanging of the twentieth century. Derek, who was nineteen, epileptic with a mental age of eleven, had been taking part in a robbery with his sixteen-year-old friend Christopher Craig, who had a gun. When confronted by the police, Derek told Christopher to 'Let him have it, Chris.' Opinion was split between those who believed that Derek was telling his friend to give up the gun and those who felt that he was telling Christopher to shoot the policeman, who died at the scene. Christopher was under the permitted age for hanging but Derek was not. Half a century would pass before Bentley was post-humously pardoned. Allegedly Bentley's defence barrister said privately, 'I think both little fuckers ought to swing.' Just as bad was the hanging of Ruth Ellis. Her lover, David Blakely, had caused her to miscarry their child after he beat her. This prompted her to kill him and she was hung on 30 July 1955. It would be another nine years before the final hanging in Britain.

Even more gruesome were the crimes detailed at the trial of John Christie, who lived at 10 Rillington Place in Notting Hill and who admitted killing at least seven and perhaps eight women including Beryl Evans. Like Bentley, he was hanged in 1953. Unfortunately, when Beryl was murdered back in 1950, her husband Timothy Evans was hung for the murder of his wife and baby, but Timothy didn't have to wait as long as Bentley for his posthumous pardon. The simple truth is that some juries are bound to make the wrong decision and while you can compensate someone who has been wrongly imprisoned, there is nothing you can do for someone who has been hanged. If the Labour government of 1964 hadn't abolished hanging, the Birmingham Six would all have gone to their graves instead of being wrongfully imprisoned for killing 21 people by planting bombs at two Birmingham pubs in 1974. They were released 1990, once the truth came out that they hadn't been behind the bombings.

But abolishing hanging hasn't reduced killing. I now live just a couple of streets away from Melrose Avenue where Dennis Nilsen dismembered young men and flushed their body parts down the drain, before he moved to Crouch End and did the same, with a total body count of fifteen. He was tried and imprisoned in 1983.

CHAPTER THREE

The Sixties

After years of sitting around listening to the radio and playing games like cards and draughts, we found that TV took over our evenings. If anything, it was the American programmes that captured our attention the most, as we watched *Gunsmoke*, *The Beverly Hillbillies*, *77 Sunset Strip* and *Perry Mason*. When I started work, we'd all sit around in the morning break talking about what we'd watched the night before.

What really transformed the impact of TV came at the beginning of the 1960s when, for the first time, we could get live coverage from the USA via satellites, which had been launched. This had a huge impact on politics as we watched the horrific levels of racism in the USA. Just a few years before, in the 1950s, an average of thirteen black men were lynched by the Ku Klux Klan every year. White Americans did not shake hands with black Americans, but black Americans had to take off their hats when they

encountered whites. Although racism was still pretty prev-
alent in Britain, it was dwarfed by the institutional racism
incorporated in America's laws. We'd seen on the television
news Arkansas Governor Orval Faubus sending 270 troops
to stop nine black kids getting into Little Rock Central
High School in 1957. This was a few years after schools
were desegregated, meaning it was now against the law to
force black and white students to go to separate schools.
We'd watched the nine o'clock news showing President
Eisenhower announcing he was sending troops to Arkansas
to protect the rights of the black students and footage showing white students cursing and spitting on those troops. This
did not stop the re-election of Faubus the following year,
but it was appalling when he announced he was closing all
schools in Little Rock as his way of preventing integration.

It wasn't just the schools; it was also the lunch counters
in Woolworth's in the US, where blacks were segregated
from whites. When black students organised sit-ins at
'whites only' lunch counters, Woolworths closed its store.
Second only to the Cold War, racism came to dominate our
news, as we watched Martin Luther King being arrested in
Georgia for protesting against racial segregation in 1963.
But it was the newly elected President Kennedy's younger
brother Robert who phoned the local judge and persuaded
him to release King. Now we all sat gripped, watching the
live coverage of the massive demonstrations against racism
in the USA. President Kennedy then introduced bills to
make racism illegal and eventually these became law after
his assassination in 1963.

Kennedy was deeply worried about the world's

perception of the USA, as audiences around the world watched a quarter of a million Americans marching against racism in Washington, including musicians Joan Baez, Bob Dylan and Peter, Paul and Mary. But the racism continued in September 1963 when four small black girls were killed when a bomb went off in their local church in Birmingham, Alabama.

These broadcasts from the US allowed us to compare the charismatic young men in Kennedy's new administration with the ageing and doddery British Prime Minister Harold Macmillan and his successor, Sir Alec Douglas-Home, who was sixty when he became prime minister. Douglas-Home had been a member of the House of Lords, and had to renounce his peerage and return to the Commons in a by-election. He told journalists that he used matchsticks when trying to work out economic problems, which immediately led him to being described as the 'matchsticks premier', perceived as out of date and out of touch. We were, of course, switching our loyalties to the bright young Harold Wilson, who was promising that if he became prime minister, he would unleash a wave of new technology and modernise Britain. After his election in 1964, he began a series of speeches about the New Britain. Tony Benn, who was Postmaster General in Wilson's new government, said Labour would pursue 'regeneration with a spiritual flavour and a suggestion of youth about it'.

The influence of television in those days was so different from now because we were all just watching the same two channels – BBC One (joined by BBC Two in 1964) and ITV –and the impact of that was captured by the comments of philosopher Marshall McLuhan, who said that TV was creating a global village, and he was certainly right. But although politics dominated our conversations at work, the 1960s generation was being transformed by the music we were hearing, from Bob Dylan's *Times They Are a-Changin'*, to the Beatles, the Stones, the Supremes and all the others. We watched in January 1967 as 20,000 hippies took over the Golden Gate Park in San Francisco as flower power gained momentum. We watched in wonder the people with their long hair taking LSD and the women removing their bras. But all that was dwarfed a couple of years later by Woodstock, where, although it rained heavily, half a million people danced to Janis Joplin, Jefferson Airplane and Jimi Hendrix as they openly smoked weed and took LSD, while some ran around naked in the mud and had sex while being filmed.

Lots of the UK's new bands grew up in London or moved to London, which was the hub of the music industry. It remains so, with many iconic songs having been written about London: 'London's Burning' by the Clash and the Kinks' 'Waterloo Sunset'. Boy George, the Eurythmics, Kate Bush, the Prodigy, Suede and Daffy are among the many whose music was influenced by London. Decades after the initial music boom of the 1960s, I was delighted to be asked to get involved with Blur on a track from The Great Escape, Blur's 1995 album. Damon Albarn had written the song 'Ernold Same' and wanted someone with a really boring voice to narrate it. They first approached Prime Minster John Major, but fortunately he refused and so they chose me. I was lucky enough to perform it at the Meltdown festival on the South Bank in 1998. The festival was curated by Scott Walker, my favourite male singer, but unfortunately I didn't get to meet him, as he was famously withdrawn, and stayed in his dressing room behind the stage.

An amazing new generation was changing our lives and our politics. In 1960, Arnold Wesker and the trade unions cooperated in cultural activity, which led to the opening of the Roundhouse in Chalk Farm, a venue that went on to stage Kenneth Tynan's shocking new play full of nudity *Oh! Calcutta!* In 1961 Peter Cook, Alan Bennett, Jonathan Miller and Dudley Moore launched the great satire *Beyond The Fringe*, which ran for four years. *Private Eye* suddenly appeared in our newsagents and stand-up political satire was launched at the Establishment club in Greek Street. This went on to have its impact on television the following year, when twenty-three-year-old David Frost launched *That Was The Week That Was* on the BBC. The Tories got the BBC to stop the programme after just over a year because they feared it would do damage to the government in the run-up to the general election in 1964.

Change was in the air in the sixties and writers were at the forefront, starting with Joseph Heller's *Catch-22*, about the madness in the Second World War. In 1962 Rachel Carson launched the debate about ecology with her amazing *Silent Spring*, which put the issue of pesticides and pollution into public debate, and the following year Betty Friedan gave birth to modern feminism with the publication of *The Feminine Mystique*. Also in 1962, Helen Gurley Brown published *Sex and the Single Girl*, starting the first public debate about sexual liberation. Films were also having an impact, with Stanley Kubrick's *Doctor Strangelove* (1964) and seeing Dustin Hoffman for the first time in 1967's *The Graduate*, the same year that *Bonnie and Clyde* came out. Even more controversial was the drug-taking in *Easy Rider*, which featured Peter Fonda, Denis Hopper and Jack Nicholson getting wasted.

By the time I started work in 1962 I was still small and with a rather nasal, whiney voice, so there was never a time any girl was attracted to me. My obsession with reptiles, amphibians and astronomy did nothing to help, as they never brought me into contact with young women. It was only when I eventually started going out with a daughter of one of my mum's friends that I learned how to kiss girls, as we spent hours lying in the park snogging. Most of my friends had got married in their late teens and had had their first sex, but it was only when I was twenty-one, at a completely drunken New Year's Eve party, that I finally lost my virginity. Perhaps if I could have afforded to go to nightclubs it might have happened a bit sooner.

While the post-war period's economic boom saw full employment and massive council house building, Britain was still a deeply conservative society when it came to the issues of sex, race and women's rights. There was never any discussion about sex at school or at home. Nothing sexually explicit was ever depicted in the cinema or on television. It was not until 1967 that the BBC for the first time broadcast a play in which a black man was seen kissing a white woman, and that was just a couple of years after our banks dropped the rule that a woman could only open a bank account if she had a letter of permission from her husband. Bank clerks were also treated badly. They had to get permission from their bank manager before they could marry, and could only live in a home approved by the bank and each year they were vetted for their appearance.

Most of us didn't even know homosexuality existed, because all our parents ever told us was 'don't ever start talking to dirty old men'. The Home Secretary, Sir David Maxwell Fyfe, told the House of Commons in 1953, 'Homosexuals in general are exhibitionists and proselytisers and a danger to others, especially the young,' and launched a real crackdown on gay men. Back in 1938 there were just 130 convictions for 'sodomy' (sex between men that included penetration); this now soared to 670 a year, and over the same period convictions for 'gross indecency' (sex between men that didn't include penetration) soured from 320 to 1,686. In 1953 actor Sir John Gielgud was fined £10 for persistent importuning, and 'dirty queer' was scrawled on the posters outside the theatre where he was performing, but there was a standing ovation as he walked out onto the stage. That same year comedian Benny Hill unleashed a furore when he used the term 'home away, home away' on the BBC, a vague reference to homosexuality. The War Office denounced it as in 'deplorable taste', as the programme had been broadcast from the Nuffield Centre for Servicemen.

In 1954 Lord Montagu of Beaulieu, his cousin Michael Pitt-Rivers and the *Daily Mail*'s Peter Wildeblood were all arrested and subsequently charged with 'conspiracy to initiate acts of gross indecency', a charge that had not been used since Oscar Wilde's prosecution in the 1890s. That same year the Admiralty issued an order to all naval officers that they should check their underlings' jars of hair gel and Vaseline for traces of pubic hair. Gay men in prison were often given electric-shock treatment and a sex hormone to try and make them straight. Each year writer and actor Dirk Bogarde went to hospital for aversion therapy, while others, like Gilbert Harding (the BBC's most popular broadcaster), hid their sexuality. Harding pretended to be on the verge of marriage to Nancy Spain, who was actually a lesbian. In 1955 the Tory MP Edward Heath was warned by police to stop his 'cottaging' (frequenting public toilets for sex with strangers). Fortunately the police kept this secret, otherwise he would never have gone on to become prime minster in 1970.

I was lucky to grow up in a house where my dad treated my mum as his equal, which wasn't usual in those days, when women were seen as there just to look after the home and do the shopping, cooking and cleaning. A study of 6,000 women in 1956 asked if they had sexual satisfaction in their marriage. Only 43 per cent said 'a lot', 36 per cent said okay, 16 per cent said 'only a little', and 5 per cent said that had no satisfaction. The mid-1950s were a very different world from now, as 95 per cent of people got married. By 1995 that had fallen to 67 per cent. There were only 7,000 divorces in 1939 but that had risen to 6,000 by 1947. A Gallup poll at the time revealed that only a quarter of us believed a divorce should be allowed by simple agreement, and until the mid-1950s anybody who got divorced got dropped off the royal garden party invite list.

A big story concerning divorce was of course that of Princess Margaret, who had wanted to marry Group Captain Peter Townsend in 1953. Townsend was divorced. The headline in *The People* newspaper broke the press silence on the matter with 'They Must End it Now'. Townsend was sent to work in Brussels for two years, but a poll conducted by the *Daily Mirror* showed 70,000 of its readers thought they should be allowed to marry and just 3 per cent were opposed. Another poll, this time by Gallup, showed 59 per cent thought they should be allowed to marry and 17 per cent said they shouldn't. But the establishment didn't agree and when Townsend returned to the UK, the cabinet met and decided that if they did marry, Margaret would lose her right of succession and her civil list allowance. Over a dinner with the Archbishop of Canterbury she was firmly told the Church was totally opposed. *The Times*, in a long and bitter editorial, dismissed public support, which was the final straw for Margaret and Townsend, and they gave up. Another bizarre example of our attitude to women was beginning to change was revealed when the ban on married women teaching was lifted by the London County Council (LCC) in 1949, but Barclays Bank would continue to refuse to employ married women until 1961.

But then all that began to change as the sixties came along. My view of London changed when I started work as an animal technician at the Royal Marsden's cancer research unit in the Fulham Road in 1962. Having grown up south of the river, where the roads were wider and the buildings less tall, north London seemed very different, and much more compressed. The other amazing change was that I started to use the Underground. In those days there were only twenty-seven Tube stations south of the river and so we all planned our lives around overground train timetables or waiting for the bus. Now I got off the train at Victoria station and jumped on the Tube, where one came along every couple of minutes.

At every tea break at work we all sat around talking about the day-by-day revelations of the Profumo scandal. The press was filled with accounts that Defence Secretary John Profumo had been having an affair with Christine Keeler, who was also having sex with a Russian agent. But what people found even more shocking was that she was white, but after her brief affair with Profumo had relationships with two black men. Half a century later, when I was London Mayor, I met Profumo, who had spent the rest of his life working for the poor in the East End. I was incredibly impressed with what a nice man he was.

Racism was pretty endemic in our society back in those days. In the late 1950s police officers would come back from patrol and write up reports that they had seen a white woman out with a black man, warning that such a relationship was 'dangerous' and that black men 'were cunning, unprincipled crooks ... accosting decent white women'. In 1952 the Bishop of Birmingham warned that some parts of his city had become 'semi-foreign areas' and three years later a woman named Gladys Langford wrote 'the number of negroes and coloured people about is amazing'. In fact, net migration figures from the West Indies had risen from 2,000 in 1953 to 30,000 in 1956, with only 5,500 coming from India, and 2,000 from Pakistan. Carmel Jones, who had come from the West Indies in 1955, wrote that he had 'gone to church ... so elated ... but after the service the vicar said he would be delighted if I didn't come back, as his congregation is uncomfortable in the company of black people.' When the *Daily Sketch* polled its readers, 81 per cent wanted to stop all immigrants coming here.

If I had come home with a black girlfriend in the 1960s the whole street would have been talking about it. But things have changed dramatically. My granddaughter is mixed race and it is just not an issue with anyone.

British Rail had a policy of telling all black applicants that jobs had been filled and, of course, in 1964 Labour would lose Smethwick in Birmingham, one of our safest seats, to the Tory candidate Peter Griffiths, running on the slogan 'If you want a nigger for a neighbour, vote Labour'. But not everyone was racist. The following year, when Martin Luther King came to London to give a sermon at St Paul's, over 4,000 people turned up to hear him. It was only in 1966, during the August Bank Holiday, that the first Notting Hill Carnival happened and gave us Londoners the chance to see the dynamism of black culture. By the late 1970s London had 1 million black and Asian residents, speaking 160 different languages, and by 2000 there would be 300 different languages in our city. I doubt if any other city in the world has been so transformed.

Fortunately, the 1964 election of a Labour government saw the beginning of change, when the progressive Home Secretary Roy Jenkins began rolling back our conservative attitudes by supporting legislation to tackle racism, give women the right to abortion (1967), abolish hanging (1964) and legalise homosexuality (1967). Homosexuality might have become legal, but we still had a long way to go before it became acceptable. Even up until the late 1970s, if an MP was outed as gay they either immediately resigned or didn't seek re-election. I was really proud that it was the London MP Chris Smith who became the first ever MP to come out in the mid-1980s. I think his courage played a big part in changing our attitudes.

In the 1960s our clothes changed as fashion blossomed. After the war nothing could ever be thrown away and we wore our clothes until they fell apart. Everything was constantly repaired and we wore it until it fell off. We also didn't have many clothes: each Sunday I would be given a pair of socks and a pair of pants that I would wear for the whole of the next week! I was working just round the corner from the King's Road in Chelsea, and some lunch-times I would just spend the hour walking along the road, looking at the fabulous clothes on sale and some of the amazing stuff men and women were wearing as they walked by me on the street. I couldn't afford any of it, so I stuck to my outfit of boring trousers and jacket. An odd comparison to the way we live today is when I think back to going out with my brother-in-law and his mates on a pub crawl every Friday night in 1965. We would all dress up in suits and ties with little white handkerchiefs stuck in our breast pockets as we went from pub to pub in Wandsworth and Lambeth.

Another incredible change was our food. Growing up in a post-war Britain, food rationing was grim because we were each allowed just 1 oz (25 g) of bacon a week and 3 lbs (1.4 kg) of potatoes, and you had to take coupons into shops in order to get rationed food, including bread and sweets. Rationing finally ended in 1954. Not surprisingly, we almost never saw anybody who was overweight then. The food choices were very limited, but slowly new items started appearing and I can remember my nan coming home in the late 1940s saying, 'The greengrocer says there will be bananas next week.' Before then I'd never seen one. And a few years later my sister and I watched in amazement as Dad produced a coconut and used a hammer to break into the shell.

As almost no one had a fridge, Mum would go shopping daily, but most of our meat was New Zealand lamb and the occasional rabbit. Mum always felt it was important to boil food long enough to make sure we wouldn't get ill, and so she would put the cabbage on at nine on Sunday morning and by the time we had it for lunch it was a nice green sludge. Around Christmastime it was possible to buy a chicken and by the late 1950s you could also get one at Easter. Apart from working men's cafés, the only other takeaway food you could buy was wonderful fish and chips. There had only been four Indian restaurants in the whole country in 1945, but when Sheikh Mohammad opened the Shah restaurant in Euston in 1952 you had to queue for half an hour before you could get a table. The following year Italian actress Gina Lollobrigida opened the Moka coffee shop in Soho, and in the same year Wimbledon saw the first Wimpy burger bar open.

The world of food began to change in 1965 when Pizza Express, the first pizza restaurant, opened in London, but when a Chinese restaurant opened on Streatham High

Road in the early 1960s, and Mum and Dad asked me if I wanted to join them for a meal there, I said no. I was horribly conservative about my food choices. Ten years later all that had changed, as my girlfriend and I would go to so many different restaurants, eating foods from all over the world. Another big impact on our food options was the government's decision to move the fruit and veg market from Covent Garden to Nine Elms in 1974. This had the effect of transforming Covent Garden into one of the best places to visit if you want a good meal.

An amazing change in London was our skyline. In 1962 the twenty-six-storey Shell building opened on the South Bank and three years later the Post Office Tower, 620 feet tall. I remember in 1971 actually going to see Centrepoint, which had just been completed. By 1981 the fifty-two-storey NatWest Tower had been built, the tallest building in Europe, although it has since been overtaken by many others, including the Shard, which has been London's tallest building since 2010

CHAPTER FOUR

London's Regeneration

Post-war Britain was physically defined by the bombing of London. Just a couple of months after the surrender of France to Germany in 1940, the first bombing of London began on 25 August, but then 400 planes began bombing our docks on the night of 7 September and that continued for fifty days. With amazing courage, the pilots in our Spitfires prevented much greater damage and their heroism inspired Churchill's great speech about our finest hour. Londoners in huge numbers – 177,000 – started taking shelter in seventy-nine Tube stations and by 1942 the government had built and opened deep shelters. People who owned a garden were given the materials by the government to build a shelter in their own backyard. My mum so hated being in them overnight, she decided to take the risk of staying in my nan's flat rather than staggering down to the shelters.

Bombing continued on and off throughout the war.

On 21 January 1944, 447 planes bombed London. A bigger shock came on 13 June when, in broad daylight, the V-1 flying bombs (nicknamed doodlebugs) started crashing down on London at about one hundred per day, with the worst causalities being on 18 Jun,e when a V-1 hit Wellington Barracks, killing 119 people. I still think of these bombs every day as I open the front door in my Victorian terraced street and see the small council estate that was built opposite after a V-bomb dropped, tragically at midday, just as all the local children had come home from nearby Mora School to get their lunch.

When you look at the pattern of where the doodle-bugs landed, it was mainly in the suburbs. Boroughs like Croydon saw 1,000 of their homes destroyed and yet the Germans had been planning for the bombs to drop on our docks and undermine our economy. What the Germans launching the bombs didn't know was that the German spies, hidden in London, who were telling them where the doodlebugs were landing, were lying, because we had managed to capture every one of those spies and instruct-ing them to send back false information. Perhaps it was one of the most appalling decisions the wartime government had to make, but to preserve our docks was vital, and so they decided to con the Germans into dropping the bombs on our suburbs. So you had a government led by a Conservative prime minister taking the decision that these bombs would largely fall on safe Conservative seats in the suburbs and the Home Counties.

Another shock followed on 8 September when the first V-2 hit Chiswick. This was the first ballistic missile in history and in the months that followed 518 hit London, killing 2,724 people before the last fell in March 1945, just a few weeks before the end of the war. We now know that German scientists had not just been working on the V-bombs, they had also been working on the atom bomb. They doubted it would ever be possible to make an atomic bomb, so they stopped working on it when Hitler's government decided to invade Poland in 1939. Instead they concentrated on developing V-bombs. Thank God, or we could have seen atom bombs dropping on London in the last days of the war.

The impact of the bombing on our housing was stunning, with one in six of all London homes damaged or destroyed. Across London, squatters were living illegally in semi-derelict buildings, while others lived in caravans, waiting to get permanent accommodation. Sadly, some would still be waiting fifteen years later. A quarter of all homes in Stepney and a third at Elephant and Castle had been damaged, and this had happened all over London, including the suburbs. In Stepney, by the end of the war 60 per cent of families were sharing housing and in Poplar that figure reached 73 per cent. Even in 1971, when I became the chair of the housing management committee on Lambeth Council, we still had council blocks in which all the tenants had to share one toilet at each end of the balconies.

The response of the London County Council (LCC) was to start buying up the bombed areas and launching a massive council-house-building programme. By May 1946 4,500 prefabs had been built and another 5,500 were under construction. Although the prefabs were only supposed to last ten years, some were standing forty years later, and the tenants often didn't want to leave because they had been the best homes in their lives. Even more significant was the impact of the LCC's plan to move 1 million Londoners out to new towns being built on the other side of the green belt.

Fortunately, the LCC had started planning the reconstruction of London two years before the end of the war, and a year later Patrick Abercrombie, the town planner advising the government, published his Greater London Plan, which included not just the new towns but five ring road motorways for London. The plan was that London's 1939 population of over 8.5 million should be reduced to 5.5 million by 1990. This policy was changed in the mid-1970s when the GLC realised London was losing too many people and jobs, and faced decline.

While lots of people believe we live in a crowded city, the truth is we have about the same population as Paris and New York, but we cover twice the space of those two cities. Two thirds of London is green space or water, and 5 per cent of London is woodland. One third of that green space is our gardens, one third parks and sports fields and the last third wildlife habitats. As pesticides and fertilisers being used by our farmers have caused so much damage to our countryside, London has become a refuge for wildlife, and we now have a more diverse wildlife than much of our countryside. We have 300 species of birds, 1,500 species of flowering plants and even ten species of bat, all finding life in our city easier than in the country. We have thirty-five species of mammal (including dolphins and seals, because the Thames is now cleaner). Sadly, we only have a few amphibians and reptiles, but London has become the stronghold of Britain's largest beetle, the stag beetle, whose population is under threat outside London. I remember I was still at school when I caught my first stag beetle; my mum was horrified I was keeping it as a pet in the house.

For those interested in nature, London has wonderful options. Just five minutes' walk from Kings Cross station will bring you to Camley Street Natural Park, which was opened by the GLC in 1985. It is awash with frogs and toads, and teaches thousands of kids every year about the natural world. The place I visit the most is the Welsh Harp Brent Reservoir near where I live, where my Labrador Coco always seems to regret that she can't splash out into the water and chase the great crested grebes, cormorants, herons and terns.

There's Rainham Marshes near Aveley to the east of London, which used to be a rifle range, but since 2000 has been overseen by the RSPB and is now swarming with birds and water voles. Many of the barges we used for the invasion of Europe on D-Day were deployed for flood defence in this area after the great flood of 1953. Sixty-five years on, those barges are now festooned with plants and are a winter home for pipits. The most recently opened nature reserve in London is Walthamstow Wetlands, home to dozens of species, including voles and pipistrelle bats.

In Barnes, back in 2000, Sir David Attenborough opened the London Wetlands Centre. Four old concrete reservoirs had become a 105-acre site with a great visitor centre and amazing views. Over 108 species of bird and 400 species of butterfly and moth can be found there. Not far away at Richmond Park you can see both the red and the fallow deer, and speckled and oak bush crickets hiding away among the rhododendrons. At Duckwood near Harold Hill every spring there is probably the most amazing sweep of bluebells anywhere in London, also a great home for badgers. Darland's Lake Nature Reserve is a protected area where the delicately beautiful snakeshead fritillary grows.

Staines Reservoirs, has vast numbers of water birds and several species of duck, although it is close to Heathrow Airport. Recently Wilson's phalarope and Baird's sandpiper have appeared there. Or course one of the most amazing sights in London is the Royal Botanic Gardens at Kew, which suffered terrible damage in the great storm of October 1987 but remains one of the most incredible places to stroll around for a day. I have, over the years, taken the children there many times, with their favourites being the woodland walkway up among the trees and the huge glass Victorian greenhouses, where dizzying iron platforms allow them to run around, looking down on the top of the plants.

If you like orchids, go to Salt Box Hill by the North Downs, which, during the first five years it was being run by the London Wildlife Trust, saw the number of invertebrate species double to 185. Most of our cemeteries have also become havens for wildlife and down at Norwood Cemetery, close to where I grew up, you can watch fox cubs come out to play in the evening. You can also spend a wonderful day cruising on London's canals and more and more Londoners are now choosing to live on canal boats.

Nowadays my local park is Gladstone Park, named after the former Liberal prime minister William Gladstone. Back in the 1880s, the area were I now live was just farmland and on the top of the hill, which is now the centre of the park, lived Lord Aberdeen, who owned the imposing Dollis Hill House. He made his home available to Gladstone throughout that decade and Gladstone loved staying there. He used it as his country retreat from 1882 to 1896, just two years before he died at the age of eighty-eight. Given all the stress that comes with being prime minister, he found the house relaxing and loved the fresh air away from all the noise of central London. He amassed his own library and used to lie in the hammock reading. He would also often have a swim in the pond, which is still there.

A few years later the American writer Mark Twain stayed there for a few weeks and wrote that 'Dollis Hill comes nearer to being a paradise than any other home I have occupied,' when he stayed at the house with his family in the summer of 1900. He went on to add that he had, 'Never seen any place that was so satisfactorily situated with its noble trees and stretch of country, and everything that went to make life delightful, and all within a biscuit's throw of the metropolis of the world.' During the First World War the mansion became a hospital for convalescing ex-servicemen. Brent Council kept it open as a café, but it was a bit run-down and needed a lot of work. Before the Labour council could get it repaired, it was burned down, and one of the Tory councillors who had opposed spending money on doing it up privately bragged he'd set off the fire.

Nowadays, the view from the top of the hill is still truly amazing, as you can see all the way south to the end of London, as far as Kent and Surrey, with the impressive view of Wembley Stadium's huge arch much closer. Walking the dog or taking the kids to the park, its history strikes me, and I try to imagine what the farmland and original house would be like if it was still standing.

Although Dollis Hill House burned down, fortunately the local stables survived and are now home to an exhibition space and a nice little café where you can get delicious home-made cakes with a fresh cup of coffee. The ducks and occasional herons who live in the huge pond on the hill often come and visit the pond in my back garden for a change of scenery.

Just a few metres north of Gladstone Park stands Chartwell Court on Brook Road, London NW2, once a large office block, now converted into flats. At the beginning of the Second World War, when we feared German forces would sweep across the Channel, the basement of this office block was adapted so Churchill and his cabinet could be housed there safely. If the Germans continued to advance, the plan was that Churchill's government would be flown to Canada, where they would be a government in exile. The bunker still remains in its original state and is open twice a year for a full tour. It houses a map room, cabinet room and offices, all forty feet below ground and protected by a five-foot-thick concrete roof.

In just one lifetime, London's coal-polluted atmosphere has been transformed, and the Thames, once devoid of all life because of pollution and sewage, is home to a huge variety of wildlife. Today, London is a haven for all forms of plants and animals, and we should all be proud of that. Back in the 1950s and 1960s, the banks of the Thames were exposed as black, stinking sludge each time the tide went out, and just over sixty years ago the Thames was declared biologically dead. Now we have 125 different species of fish and frequent visits from harbour seals and grey seals. Back in the Middle Ages the occasion whale would swim up the Thames, though sadly they were captured and eaten, with a seventy-foot whale providing dinner for many back in 1308.

The peregrine falcon, which was almost wiped out by the pesticide DDT back in 1962, now has sixty-eight pairs in the UK, but some of them have left the cliffs and mountains and moved to London to live on our tall buildings, where they swoop down on pigeons at 250 kilometres per hour – the world's fastest bird.

Even more bizarre is the fact that London has become a home for over 10,000 Indian rose-ringed parakeets. It's believed that they bred from a few escaped pets, but I was also once told they had been used in the filming of *The African Queen* at Shepperton Studios and were released afterwards.

Cormorants first arrived in London to breed in 1987 and hundreds now live at Walthamstow Wetlands. And of course, right in the heart of London, in Regent's Park, you can watch the herons and the tawny owls, the most common owl in London. You can also get pecked at by the huge number of pelicans that throng Green Park.

The impact of climate change means many animals and

birds are moving north and being replaced by ones coming from the warmer south, so change is going to continue much more rapidly.

If you want to learn more about London's wildlife, I recommend *Wild London: The Nature of a Capital* by Iain Green.

CHAPTER FIVE

History

If we had a time machine and could go back 50 million years, we wouldn't be able to see any part of London, as all of southern England was submerged beneath the sea. Millions of years later, the sea receded, leaving the deposit of London clay on which our city is now built. Popping back into the time machine and turning up just half a million years ago, what is now London was covered by ice, with mammoths and woolly rhinos being hunted down by an early human species of hunter-gatherers, using crude tools.

One hundred and twenty thousand years ago London had been transformed once more into a warm paradise for hippos, elephants and crocodiles. Twelve thousand years ago it was another cold era of ice, with reindeer, horses and woolly rhinos being killed and eaten by our ancestors. Eight thousand years ago the Thames then was two metres higher than it is today, and around 11,500 years ago saw the ending of the Ice Age, which led to Britain being cut off from Europe by the English Channel, a legacy that dominates our politics today.

We know little about our ancestors living in London in ancient times, but we have discovered a wooden bridge built at Vauxhall sometime between 1285 BC and 1750 BC. By 1600 BC some of London's land had been taken over by farmers living in ring forts and trading in bronze. But then locally produced iron led to a collapse of trade contacts and saw the decline of London's settlements.

In 55 BC, as we are all taught at school, Julius Caesar invaded us but then withdrew. His records do name our river the Thames. The second invasion followed in 43 AD, when Brits were chased across the Thames by the Roman armies, with some soldiers travelling on their elephants. The Romans then built their first dwellings and began a reign that would last for 360 years. Their Londinium settlement was founded in 50 AD, with the first bridge across the Thames. It was rebuilt a number of times, most recently in 1973 and is known as London Bridge. London became the port for supplies, armies and trade for the whole country as the Romans started building the road network throughout the rest of Britain. Those roads are still with us today. I remember this each time I walk along Kilburn High Road or Cricklewood Broadway, knowing I am walking on a road nearly 2,000 years old. We would struggle to recognise the Thames in those days, as it was six times wider than it is today between Southwark and the City, with most of the area being marshes.

In 60 AD, Queen Boudicca led a rebellion against the Romans and as the governor Suetonius fled, most Londoners were crucified, hanged or burned to death as the city was burned down. Eventually the Romans defeated Boudicca, who poisoned herself, and rebuilt London as their trading centre for manufactured goods from Europe and the Middle East. To protect the city a twenty-foot wall was erected, surrounded by a six foot ditch built in 190 AD.

Until the Emperor Constantine became a Christian in 312 AD, Londoners worshipped the Persian god Mithras. We know this because back in 1954 the Temple of Mithras was excavated near the underground Walbrook River, close to Cannon Street station. Just a few years later, in 367 AD, the Scots, Picts and Saxons attacked and ransacked London. A new Roman army arrived, recaptured the city and changed its name to Augusta, the name of the then emperor. But in 410 AD Emperor Honorius decided to withdraw from Britain and little is known of what happened to us in the next two hundred years, except that Germans arrived here in large numbers.

Clearly, being dropped from the Roman Empire was not a disaster, because 320 years later, in 730 AD, Bede describes London as 'a metropolis ... of many peoples coming by land and sea'. Vikings arrived to slaughter most Londoners in 842 and again in 851, then the Danes occupied London in 871, but were defeated by the armies of Wessex in 886 under King Alfred. The violence started again in 994 when Danes and Norwegians attacked London and won control by 1013. King Ethelred the Unready recaptured London in 1014 but his Saxon regime ended in 1066 when William of Normandy won the Battle of Hastings. Interestingly, William did not attack London, but signed a deal in which

Londoners agreed to his rule and he allowed them to retain their privileges and status. To protect his reign he began building the Tower of London while London's population boomed to somewhere between 10,000 and 15,000 in the following years.

The horrors caused by these endless wars were almost matched by our weather in the centuries to come. The much wider Thames was often so shallow that you could walk across it and in 1114 and 1158 the Thames ran dry. In the winter of 1410 the Thames was frozen for fourteen weeks, followed by floods at Barking and Dagenham in 1462. In March of 1625 floods overwhelmed Westminster Hall, leaving it under three feet of water.

Hurricanes were an occasional problem, with many London buildings demolished in 1362. In 1703 massive numbers of buildings were wrecked, ships were sunk and many people were left dead. The great gale of 1752 also demolished many buildings and lifted two ships out of the river at Vauxhall and dumped them on land. Eleven years later a four-foot-deep flood swamped the city and another great flood in 1791 forced lawyers to have to row boats to get to the courts in the City. In 1813 and 1814 from 27 December to 3 January a great fog forced people to stay in their homes, while the Thames was frozen from 23 December into February.

The impact of Londoners on their environment became clear in 1858 during the Great Stink. During this hot summer the smell of raw sewage in the Thames became so awful that members of the Houses of Parliament insisted on perfume-saturated curtains to cover the windows.

Parliament responded more rapidly than it does these days and, within seven years, 1,300 sewers had been built to take the sewage down river, although it remained polluted by factory waste.

Another one of the horrors of living in London in the past came from the fires created by a crowded and cramped city with wooden buildings back to back. The list of fires is too many to report, but 1077 saw the first great fire and in 1212 3,000 people died in an inferno.

The cramped buildings didn't just lead to endless fires but helped the rapid spread of disease and in 1117 we opened our first leprosy hospital, with St Bart's hospital following in 1123, and in 1148 St Katharine by the Tower, a hospital for the poor.

To make matters worse, poor old Londoners had to put up with the occasional earthquake. On 13 February 1247 many homes collapsed and this happened again in 1275, and in 1580 an apprentice was killed by falling masonry. The Bishop of London explained why this was happening following an earthquake in 1750, when he warned that God was 'punishing Londoners for their depravity'.

All these problems were dwarfed by the spread of famine and disease in such a tiny, crowded city with no cures available. In 1348 the Black Death swept through Europe, killing a third of the population. Across Europe, Christian bigots blamed the Jews for this, which led to thousands of Jews being killed. The Black Death returned again and again: 1361, 1369, and in 1407 30,000 Londoners died. In 1499 20,000 Londoners died, with three more plagues hitting London before, in 1665, somewhere between 80,000 and 100,000 Londoners died because of the Black Death, and this was out of a population of just half a million. But it was the Great Fire of 1666 that helped to end the plague, as 13,000 homes were burned down, and the last instance of the Black Death recorded is in a case in Rotherhithe in 1679.

Although never as bad as bubonic plague, by 1832 cholera had begun to sweep through the city, killing people in just a few hours. The worst year, in which 13,000 died from cholera, was 1849. Even by 1850 in London the average lifespan was just thirty-eight years. By 1890 it had risen to forty-four, but in 1900 a study showed that the well-off living in the West End were getting to fifty-five years, while the poor in the East End were just making an average of thirty years. It's still a problem today, with the residents of Golders Green averaging seventy-eight years, but the people of Harlesden only sixty-eight years. Although the horrors of past centuries make London seem like a pretty grim place to live in, much the same was happening over most of the rest of the planet. In the Americas, over 90 per cent of all the native populations were wiped out by the diseases we brought with us on the pilgrim boats.

But London was also a brilliant hive of new ideas and inventions. After Henry I became king, he had the first public lavatory built. Under Edward VI grammar schools began, with Elizabeth II overseeing the founding of Westminster School, Enfield Grammar, Kingston, St Olave's, Merchant Taylors', Highgate Grammar, St Martin's, Harrow and Queen Elizabeth Grammar.

In 1569 London created its first lottery and seven years later opened its first theatre. The first coffee house appeared in 1652, but within twenty years the government worried that they had become a centre for political debate and tried, but failed, to shut them down. The first Turkish bath, actually run by Turks, opened in 1679, and the following year was the first time anyone could get fire insurance. In 1685 the first-ever greenhouse was built in Chelsea's Physic Garden.

Perhaps one of the most significant innovations, which would have a huge impact on our lives, came in 1694 when the Bank of England was created and given the power to tax alcohol. The first pantomime in London was staged in 1702 and the first daily paper, the *Daily Courant*, was published. Seven years later the first-ever building regulations were introduced, including the attempt to prevent fire spreading up the outside walls of buildings. I doubt if the horror of Grenfell Tower would have happened if building regulations had not been weakened as part of Thatcher's legacy.

Not everyone liked the Hackney cab trade. Back in 1660 they were banned from plying the streets, so customers had to walk to the cab ranks to find one, and two years later a £5 tax was introduced on each cab. In 1695 they were banned from Hyde Park – a ban that lasted over 200 years. The City of London Corporation brought in rules that people must drive on the left of the road to reduce the risk of a coachman hitting pedestrians with their horsewhips. In 1773 our Stock Exchange opened, preparing the way for the endless cycle of boom and bust in the centuries to follow. A more positive change came seven years later when William Addis invented the first toothbrush, made of horsehair and bone. Just three years later saw the launch of the first-ever hot-air balloon, the first manned balloon flight following in 1774.

The first public railway (drawn by horses) opened from Wandsworth to Croydon in 1803 and the first zoo was built in Regent's Park in 1826, initially devoted to research but eventually opened to the public. The Metropolitan Police was founded by Home Secretary Robert Peel in 1829 and four years later the first fire brigade was founded. London's first steam railway, which ran between Bermondsey and Deptford, opened in 1836 and six years later Queen Victoria rode on a train for the first time, from Windsor to Paddington. Kew Gardens opened in 1841 and in 1868 came the first traffic lights by the junction of Bridge Street and Great George Street in Westminster. Alexander Graham Bell demonstrated the first use of the telephone in 1876 in Brown's Hotel in Piccadilly, where my wife Emma and I spent our wedding night 133 years later. Incidentally, Brown's is also the oldest hotel in London, having being built in 1837.

Twenty years earlier a tunnelling machine had been invented and by 1890 the first Tube opened between Stockwell and King William Street. The fare was two pence. Marconi invented radio in Italy in 1895 but nobody was interested, so he came to London and did a deal with the Post Office to develop radio communications, which led to the first wireless transmission on 27 July 1896 and laid the foundations for the BBC to start regular broadcasting in 1922.

The first moving pictures were shown in 1893 in Piccadilly and this led to the opening of several cinemas in 1910, including the Ritzy in Brixton where my parents would be taking me forty years later. At Harrods the first escalator appeared in 1898 and London's first aerodrome opened at Hendon in 1911. The first proper airport began operating from London Terminal Aerodrome, Croydon in 1920, which by 1928 had become the first major civil airport in the world. Heathrow eventually replaced Croydon in 1946.

Perhaps the biggest change to the life of my generation grew from John Logie Baird, who worked in two attic rooms in Frith Street. developing the first image transmission in 1924 and two years later showing the first experimental television transmission. It would take another ten years before the BBC began its first two-hours-a-day broadcast from Alexander Palace on 2 November 1936.

I found out about all these innovations doing the research for this book and it's hard to think of any other city in the world where so many new ideas that would change our way of life came about. I believe one of the main reasons London attracted scientists, inventors and artists from around the world is because it is a great city to live in.

CHAPTER SIX

Racism

F oreign merchants had been living in London since the coming of the Romans and while this has boosted our economy, there have often been tensions and violence based on race or faith. Even before the Norman Conquest of 1066, there was a French community of wine merchants. The eleventh century saw the arrival of Danes, and Germans in the twelfth century. There was also a longstanding Jewish community, who tragically experienced centuries of bigotry. At the coronation of Richard I in 1189, Jews were banned from attending and when some turned up with gifts, a mob started killing them and the riots spread, with the killing of Jews throughout England. It was only in 1227 in Ironmonger Lane that the first synagogue was finally opened.

One of the causes of anti-Semitism was the Christian claim that it was the Jews who killed Jesus, but I suspect that another cause of anti-Semitism arose out of the decision of

Christian churches to ban bankers from ever entering their buildings. In some churches their wives and children were also banned. Some European countries then passed laws making it a crime for bankers to enter a church, so this was not just a problem in London but throughout the Christian world. This meant that back in medieval times, because Christians could not work as bankers, a disproportionate number of bankers and loan-makers (defined as usurers, who loaned money at high rates of interest) were Jewish and therefore, with the inevitable cycles of boom and bust and the occasional escalating interest rates on loans, this unfairly fuelled anti-Semitism.

At one point, Jews had to take shelter in the Tower of London in 1236, and further anti-Jewish riots occurred in 1262. In 1275 Edward I banned Jews from practising usury. Then just three years later there were claims that Jews were clipping bits of silver and gold from coins, which led to 600 being imprisoned in the Tower and 293 hanged. Seven years later, Edward closed the first synagogue. Five years after that 15,000 Jews were expelled from England, with most moving to France. Nearly four centuries later, by 1656, Oliver Cromwell had removed the ban and allowed Jewish resettlement of Britain. By 1817 a free school for Jewish children opened, and is still with us today as the Jewish Free School of Camden.

But it was not just the Jews who experienced violent prejudice. In 1326 London mobs attacked Lombard merchants (Italians of German origin) and a wave of assaults erupted in 1517 when on Easter Tuesday Canon Bell gave a sermon in Bishopsgate in which he denounced foreign merchants.

As assaults spread, a curfew was imposed and hundreds of rioters imprisoned and twenty gallows were erected across the city, with many hanged.

A census of foreigners living in London took place in 1567, showing forty Scottish residents, forty-five from Spain and Portugal, forty-five Burgundians, 140 Italians, 428 French and 2,030 Dutch. This was at a time when there were only about 100,000 people living in London. In 1593, the first wave of Irish immigrants arrived at Wapping and Queen Elizabeth I ordered them to go home, but by 1861, 178,000 Irish people had moved to London, making up a twentieth of our population.

Anti-Catholic demonstrations erupted in 1679 after Catholics were blamed for trying to burn down Clerkenwell Prison, and two years later 322 French Protestants (Huguenots) arrived, having been driven out of France by Catholics. More came over the next few years, settling in Spitalfields and Clerkenwell. The anti-Catholic Gordon Riots erupted in 1780, leaving over 450 dead or wounded. In the 18th century Catholics faced higher taxes than non-Catholics, had no access to education and were not allowed to stand for Parliament or to vote.

Anti-Semitism continued to be an issue, despite Cromwell revoking the ban on Jews living in Britain. Following the assassination of Tsar Alexander II in 1881, a new wave of Jewish refugees fled from Russia and Poland to London. In 1906 one headline in the *Daily Mail* ran 'Jews bring crime and disease to Britain' and the growth of Oswald Moseley's British Union of Fascists (BUF) in the inter-war years led to the Battle of Cable Street on 4

October 1936, when 3,000 Blackshirts (members of the BUF) marched through the East End denouncing Jews, but were blocked and turned back at Cable Street by barriers erected by Jews, socialists and communists.

After the Second World War the arrival of the Windrush Generation began to fuel a new form of racism, with four evenings of riots across London starting in Notting Hill in 1958. This racism was fuelled as many MPs started demanding a ban on Commonwealth citizens coming to Britain. The Labour leader Hugh Gaitskell opposed the legislation (which gave the government power to control immigration, rather than a complete ban) when it was introduced by the Tories in 1962, but it became law. Many of the riots that followed came from black people erupting against the discrimination and violence they had suffered. In the week before the 1981 GLC election, there were riots across London and in 1985 an unarmed black woman was shot when police raided her home. This triggered riots, with the worst in Brixton, where the police station was petrol bombed; this was followed by further riots in Peckham a few days later. On 6 October the Broadwater Farm estate in Tottenham was raided by police, triggering the riots that led to PC Keith Blakelock being hacked to death.

Our media, and not just the *Daily Mail*, have pandered to bigotry and fear for generations. At the beginning of the twentieth century it was the Jews being demonised, followed by the Irish and then, after the war, the Caribbeans. Today it has become Muslims and East Europeans. But most of the media ignore one simple fact. Seventy per cent of migrants who come to Britain have a university degree, whereas even today less than half of British children are going to university. London has received a massive intake of migrants over the years and it has had an impact on our economy. We are the only region in Europe that matches American levels of productivity and competitiveness. But politicians still talk about the threat of migration and ignore the economic reality. The claim that migrants have come here and taken our jobs and our homes overlooks two simple facts: for forty years Labour and Tory governments stopped building council housing and did nothing to intervene as 6 million jobs in manufacturing were wiped out by a lack of investment and support from governments.

An equally endemic form of discrimination was, of course, directed against women. All religions were created back in a time when women were seen as the possession of their husbands or their fathers, and this became enshrined in all religions and cultures. An amazing example of this attitude took place in Portman Market, west of Regent's Park, in 1833, when a husband arrived pulling his wife behind him with a halter round her neck to put her up for auction. She was eventually sold to a dustman for five shillings. Long after public toilets were made available for men, there continued to be total opposition to the idea that women should have access to public toilets and it was only in 1884 that the first women's toilet opened at Oxford Circus.

Throughout the Victorian era only a small proportion of men were allowed to vote because the law said you could only vote if you owned property. A series of minor reforms slowly extended the right to vote, but not to women. It was only by 1907 that Parliament passed a law allowing women to stand in local council elections and seven years later the House of Lords rejected the idea that women should have a right to vote in Parliamentary elections. What changed all this was the First World War when, as so many men were sent to fight abroad, women had to step in and fill the jobs that men had been doing for generations. This changed many men's perceptions of women, their ability and their talents, and finally, in February 1918 women aged thirty and over were given the right to vote. During that Parliament the law was changed to allow all men over twenty-one the right to vote even if they did not own property. It was only in 1928 that the law was changed to allow all women, like all men over the age over twenty-one, the right to vote.

It would still take generations to overcome prejudices against women, such as the outrage that erupted when Marie Stopes opened the first birth-control clinic in 1921. Even as late as 1973 the reactionary old aldermen on the City of London Corporation blocked the election of the first woman alderman, Edwina Coven. Two years later they gave in and accepted the election of Mary Donaldson.

CHAPTER SEVEN

The Governance of London

F or its first few centuries London's was confined to just a small area we now call the City of London. Although thousands of people came to live around the outside of the City wall, the City constantly refused to expand its boundary to include them, a policy that remains unchanged to this day. It was only in 1189 that for the first time the king allowed the creation of the post of Lord Mayor of London, filled by Henry fitz Ailwin, who served until his death in 1212.Three years later King John granted the City its royal charter and eventually, fifty-nine years later, the first town clerk was appointed. But there continued to be tensions between the monarchs and the City authorities, and Edward I abolished the mayoralty and appointed his own nominee to govern the City. This lasted thirteen years until, in exchange for a substantial sum of money to support King Edward, the City was allowed to reappoint its own mayor again.

The establishment always feared that Londoners, both those living within the City walls and those outside, were too radical and represented a threat to the great and the good. It was the Peasants' Revolt in 1381 that fed these fears. The revolt was against the imposition of the poll tax and was led by Watt Tyler. On 15 June the king and the Mayor of London met Tyler, whereupon the mayor stabbed him to death and the rebels dispersed.

Just two years before Queen Victoria assumed the throne, in 1837 at the age of eighteen, every major city except London had been given the right to elect a council. The City of London Corporation had continued to oppose any new London government for decades and it was only in 1854 that the Metropolitan Board of Works was created. But Londoners were denied the right to vote for those serving on the board. Undoubtedly the refusal to allow Londoners the right to vote for their own council had been influenced by major demonstrations in 1848, one in Trafalgar Square opposing income tax, and one a month later in April, when the Chartists marched to Parliament to demand voting reform. No sooner had the Metropolitan Board of Works been created than the following year saw bread riots across London in February, clock workers rioting in March at Whitechapel and demonstrations in June and July against the bill banning Sunday trading, which was seen as a real blow to the poorest workers, who only had time to shop on Sundays.

Not surprisingly, Karl Marx took part in the protests and believed this could be the beginning of a revolution. But it was not just Marx. London was open to every kind of political exile, including Trotsky, Lenin, and poor old Stalin, living in a cubicle in the Tower doss house. The writer Peter Ackroyd was right when he complained that, 'The East End can be considered one of the primary sites of world communism!' Violence erupted again on Bloody Sunday, 13 November 1887, when socialists marched to Westminster protesting at the imprisonment of the Irish MP William O'Brien. Two died and over a hundred were injured.

In 1870 the London School Board had been formed and elected. New permanent schools began opening in 1873. In 1871, the Liberal's proposal to create a London council was blocked and any further move towards democracy for Londoners was halted as the establishment watched with horror the violence of the Paris commune in 1871, fearing something similar could happen here.

As the years passed, the Metropolitan Board of Works, with its forty-five members, became notorious for corruption, but the decisive factor in creating the London County Council (LCC) was caused by a split in the Liberal Party, with those Liberals opposed to home rule for Ireland defecting under the leadership of Joseph Chamberlain. Those members now held the balance of power in Parliament. They were prepared to support the Tory leader Lord Salisbury in his bid to become prime minster, but to get the rebels support, Salisbury had to make several concessions, one of which was to create the LCC.

With 120 councillors and twenty aldermen, the first election in 1889 led to a Liberal socialist and radical majority who were re-elected again in 1894. The LCC was seen as such a significant body that over forty members of the House of Lords stood and got elected as councillors or aldermen. At the third election of 1895 it was a dead heat, with fifty-nine moderates (Tory) versus fifty-nine progressives, who retained power on the casting vote of the chairman. Prime Minister Lord Salisbury became increasingly worried about the radical policies of the LCC and wanted to try and undermine its powers by creating London boroughs that would take most of those powers away. Fortunately he still had to rely on the support of the rebel Liberals, so he was only able to get the twenty-eight London boroughs formed in 1900 with very limited powers. Four years later the LCC took over the London School Board.

In 1907 the Tories won a majority on the LCC and immediately the Tory obsession with abolishing the LCC vanished, but the first thing the Tories wanted was a wonderful new building to work in. The Tories appointed a twenty-nine-year-old architect, Ralph Knott, who designed the amazing County Hall, which sits opposite the House of Commons. Because of the Frist World War, building works were halted and the first phase opened in 1922. Sadly, Knott died aged fifty and never lived to see County Hall's final stages completed in 1933.

In 1933 the Tory-dominated government created the London Passenger Transport Board, which took over five railway companies, seventeen tramways and sixty-one bus companies over the decades to come. Board members were always appointed by the government, and the LCC had no influence. It was only in 1969 that Wilson's government passed a law, supported by Mrs Thatcher, who was then the

Tories' shadow transport minister, that transferred control of transport to the Greater London Council (as the LCC had become).

To everyone's surprise, in 1934 Labour won a majority on the LCC under the leadership of Herbert Morrison. He started introducing a progressive socialist agenda, which would eventually be applied to the whole country following the election of the Labour government in 1945. One of the most significant polices was a massive council-house-building programme. Within just a few years, the Tories were once more talking about the need to abolish the LCC, but with the outbreak of the Second World War that issue was dropped.

Labour continued to rule the LCC right up until its abolition in 1965. With the war out of the way, the Tories again wanted to break Labour's hold of County Hall so they established a royal commission in the 1950s to investigate changing the LCC by enlarging it by five times so it would include all the London Tory-dominated suburbs. The Tories believed that by bringing in everything from Bromley to Barnet they would guarantee the return of a Tory GLC.

Whereas the LCC had been run continuously for its first eighteen years by the Liberals and then by Tories for twenty-seven years and finally by Labour for thirty-one years, the new GLC would see a change of control at each of its six elections except one. Labour won a landslide in 1964 much to the amazement of the Tories, who then won by an even bigger landslide three years later and were re-elected in 1970. Labour took it back in 1973 (with me as the second-youngest Labour member), but after a disastrous shambles lost to the Tories in 1977 (the term had been extended from three to four years by Edward Heath's government).

Then in 1981 Labour won again, but it was a very different kind of administration. For the first time the post-war generation, who had been transformed by the culture and politics of the 1960s, were running something. While the 1960s were dominated by music, fashion and food, and my generation revelled in it all, by 1968 it became political all over the world, with mass protests and riots from Chicago to Paris and Berlin. I sat glued to the television each night, watching these events unfold. Much of the anger was fuelled by America's relentless war against the Vietnamese, but there was also the uprising in Czechoslovakia as they fought to throw off the legacy of Stalin's bureaucracy. When Bobby Kennedy announced he was running against President Johnson with a promise to end the war, I was electrified. It looked as though America was going to get a president who could make a better world, but just a few months later he had been assassinated, De Gaulle had crushed the rebellion in France, the Russians had stormed back into Czechoslovakia and all my hopes were blown away.

CHAPTER EIGHT

GLC Days

In 1973 when I first stood for the Greater London Council (GLC), the governing body for London's boroughs, my constituency of Norwood was a key marginal seat and my only opponent for the Labour nomination was Richard Balfe, now a Tory Lord. But what helped me win by a landslide was the fact that the sitting Tory member for Norwood, Peter Malynn, had voted to build a six-lane motorway through the constituency, which would have demolished 1,100 homes and blighted another 1,200. It was also going to run through our three local parks. When I called a public meeting to oppose this, 700 people turned up and we launched the campaign 'Save Norwood from the M23. Vote Livingstone' (without mentioning Labour). The Tories put out leaflets warning that I was a dreadful 'red under the bed', but it didn't stop me winning.

At the first meeting the outgoing Tory chairman of the GLC insisted on his local chaplain delivering a prayer,

although the Labour group had said we didn't think meetings should start with a prayer. The chaplain got his own
back with the shortest prayer I have ever heard: 'I have been
told to be brief, so I will simply beseech almighty God to
watch over those who have chosen to walk a crooked path.'

As a GLC member you were treated better than an MP.
We all had an office and access to typists and chauffeur-
driven cars. Our drinks cupboards were kept topped up and
if we wanted to, we could go to the Royal Box at the Royal
Festival Hall and we were all called Honourable Members
rather than mere councillors.

Oddly enough, one of my best GLC friends was the
Tory member David Avery, who had been an MI5 officer
and loved telling everyone about the time when a Special
Branch officer turned up to question him because it was
suspected that he was gay and therefore a security risk. The
allegation had come from the Tory MP Duncan Sandys,
who had decided David was gay because 'he smoked his
cigarettes like a woman'. When David finally persuaded
the officer he wasn't gay, he got the response, 'Well, I am.'

Given that the bizarre row about our airport capacity
still rolls on today, we came to power just as the construction of a new airport in the Thames Estuary, near Maplin
Sands had been proposed. The project had originally been
suggested back in the 1930s, again in the 1950s and once
more in the 1960s. Tory Prime Minister Ted Heath threw
his weight behind the scheme, promising the first runway
would open in 1976. I was delighted to see dear old Norman
Tebbit being one of those MPs who voted against it. Labour
MP Tony Crosland joked that the Maplin airport should be

called Heathrowgrad. Just a year later he was the minister in Wilson's government who scrapped the scheme.

When he was prime minister, Gordon Brown decided to build a third runway at Heathrow. By the time I became Mayor of London the British National Party was supporting the idea. When Boris Johnson became mayor he commissioned a report about the cost of building Maplin Airport, which concluded it would be at least £40 billion.

Compared with being an MP, where mainly you just talk about laws and policy, I loved the fact that at the GLC we spent our time doing things, and I began to daydream that perhaps in twenty-five or thirty years I could follow in the footsteps of Herbert Morrison and become County Hall's leader.

I was still also on my local borough council of Lambeth, but all us lefties had been forced out of chairing committees and onto the back benches, and I became even more notorious when I supported the Gay Liberation Front, which wanted a grant of £18,000 to provide an advice service. Sadly, the right-wing Labour councillor George West waged a holy war against what he called 'the sodomites'. I pointed out that in San Francisco Harvey Milk had just been elected the first openly gay politician in the USA, but West won the debate by warning that gay men 'wanted to force it down people's throats', without a hint of irony.

I was also pushed onto the back benches at the GLC when I opposed Labour ratting on its promise to cut bus and Tube fares. Jim Daly, the chair of the transport committee, proposed a motion to the Labour group that 'Ken Livingstone should not be allowed to speak at GLC meetings'. He won the vote, but I ignored it and just a few years later he quit the Labour Party to join the Social Democratic Party (SDP).

I was working closely with GLC member and future Labour MP Tony Banks, who was planning to stand for GLC leader after the next election. That meant we needed to get some more lefties on to the council and one we persuaded to stand was Greg Dyke, who sadly didn't win the Putney seat, but did go on to change the face of television with Roland Rat. In the run up to the election the *Daily Telegraph* was screaming 'Shock wave of Marxism hits GLC elections'. I got on well with Tony for years, but he was a bit embarrassed when he discovered that my dad and I had cleaned the windows of the expensive flat his parents lived in in Streatham. Tony made me promise never to tell anyone about this.

Another wonderful new ally was Kate Hoey, who had just left the International Marxist Group to join the Labour Party in Stoke Newington, where I had been selected as the Labour candidate. We immediately got on well and she loved telling me what a nightmare it was when she was the vice president of the National Union of Students under Jack Straw's presidency. She was horrified to be subjected to a smear campaign that she had been involved with the 'Stoke Newington Eight', otherwise known as the Angry Brigade, who had tried to assassinate Ted Heath's employment minister, Robert Carr. Kate begged me to give up my nomination as the Labour candidate for Hampstead at the general election when the ageing MP for Stoke Newington retired. She wanted me to be her MP, but I couldn't rat on all those good lefties who had fought to get me the

Hampstead nomination. We both had a good laugh when she got a phone call from Jack Straw asking for her support in his attempt to become Stoke Newington's MP.

A few years later, in the run-up to the 1981 GLC election, I became the candidate for the crucial marginal seat of Paddington, where the year before the local priest had denounced the Labour MP Arthur Latham because of his support for abortion. The priest died suddenly and I was quite shocked to be told that I had to attend his funeral, which was being presided over by Cardinal Basil Hume. As I entered the church I was taken to sit by the coffin, with the Tory candidate sitting on the other side. I thought this was bizarre, but it actually opened the way to a good working relationship between myself and Cardinal Hume.

In his sixteen-page manifesto for the GLC election Horace Cutler, a Tory, and leader of the GLC 1977–81, mentioned the threat of Marxism seventeen times, and the right-wing press were equally afraid. The *Daily Telegraph* ran with the headline 'Will London be Marxified?' and 'Could the dictatorship of the proletariat be imposed without a prior communist revolution?', while the *Daily Express* roared 'Why We Must Stop These Red Wreckers'.

I was surprised when an *Evening Standard* reporter asked to have a private conversation with me. He said that Cutler was renting a flat owned by London Transport above Baker Street Tube station, which he used as 'love nest', but Lord Matthews, who controlled the paper, wouldn't allow the story to run. The reporter asked me to publicly raise the issue, but I wanted to win on the basis of our policies and not dirt and smears. Shortly after this, Thames TV's Ed

Boyle told me how he had turned up to interview Cutler in his office but found the door locked. When it eventually opened, a woman rushed out while Cutler rearranged his clothing. 'Nothing like a good woman after lunch,' said Cutler, but given he was rich enough to sue, Thames TV didn't dare mention it.

As we all turned up for the count on polling day, the chair of the Paddington Tories came up to me and said, 'Our candidate's no good, so I voted for you.' His opinion might have been influenced by my defence of lesbian and gay rights, given that Conservative Ian Harvey had been forced to resign as an MP back in 1958 after he was caught in the bushes of St James's Park with a guardsman.

As the results came in, Labour had won control of County Hall by fifty seats to forty-two and at the age of thirty-five I was the youngest ever leader at the GLC. Bizarrely, that night Thatcher made a speech to the Scottish Tories. saying my plan was to 'impose upon this nation a tyranny which the peoples of Eastern Europe yearn to cast aside'. The idea that cutting fares would trigger a communist revolution was bonkers, but it didn't stop the *Sun*'s headline 'Red Ken Crowned King of London. His victory means full steam ahead red-blooded Socialism for London'. The *Daily Mail* claimed 'A left-wing extremist was installed as leader' and the *Daily Telegraph* complained that I had 'no background, no education worth speaking of, no money and had appointed a black man to chair the Police Committee'. Up until that moment, no GLC leader had been a national political figure and I doubt if 1 per cent of Brits had ever known the name of any GLC leader, but within twenty-four hours every Tory newspaper had sent a reporter in full time to County Hall. The *Daily Mail* even brought back their war correspondent from the Middle East and told him he had to submit six stories a day on the GLC.

I caused a lot of anger among some GLC members when I stopped the nonsense that included extravagant receptions at which we fed and watered the establishment and a yearly holiday abroad for the chair of the GLC, paid for by the tax payer. I also scrapped the leader's chauffeur-driven car and stopped the nonsense of the chair of the council wearing medieval clothes when greeting visiting heads of state. The porters, however, were pleased when I said they no longer had to stand to attention when I walked by.

London's police commissioner, Sir David McNee, had had regular working lunches with my Tory predecessor, but now ordered that no police officer was to have any contact with GLC members.

Given that this was back in the days of 1981, I was naïve to believe that our stand on women's rights, racism and homophobia might be fairly reported in the press, but at that time I believe not a single reporter or print worker was black, no reporter was openly gay and no woman held any position above that of editing the women's page.

Because my wife Christine and I had separated a year before the election, the press was obsessed with my support for gay rights and was soon reporting that I was importing pills from San Francisco that changed the taste of human semen to strawberry flavour. The *Daily Mail* was the worst when it claimed that three psychologists had diagnosed my behaviour as shocking, although they all denied the quotes attributed to them. The pathetic Press Council dismissed complaints made against the *Daily Mail* because of this. My first speech about lesbian and gay rights dominated the following morning's press coverage and my nephew, Terry, having finished his paper round, told my mum, 'The papers say Uncle Ken's a fairy.'

I couldn't do anything about all these lies and smears because of the cost of bringing a libel case, but when *Private Eye* ran the story that the Libyan dictator Muammar Gaddafi had put $200,000 into a secret Swiss bank account held by myself and Ted Knight, the socialist leader of Lambeth Council, Knight insisted on suing and we eventually got £10,000, which we used to fund a lefty paper.

As I spoke out about the need to end the IRA bombing campaign, which would require negotiations, the *Sun* claimed: 'Mr Livingstone steps forward as the defender and the apologist for the criminal, murderous activities of the IRA.' In the weeks that followed I was physically attacked three times on the streets. The press hysteria got worse, and my chief of staff, Bill Bush, became increasingly worried about my safety. When the Met's Special Branch came to warn us that my movements were being monitored by extremist groups, Bush asked for them to provide protection, but they refused because I lived in a small studio and travelled on public transport.

We didn't know it until the story broke several weeks later, but Lady Shirley Porter, the Tory leader of Westminster Council, had set up the 'Keep London Free' campaign. At a secret meeting on 23 October 1981, forty-five business people, including hotel magnate Sir Charles

Forte and businessmen from Cadbury Schweppes, Taylor Woodrow, GEC, Blue Circle, Tate & Lyle, J. Sainsbury, Allied Breweries, Beechams, Lazards, Ladbrokes and De La Rue contributed £200,000 to Aims of Industry, a corporate lobby group set up to oppose the nationalisation of British. Their plan, to campaign for the abolition of the GLC.. Members also included the writer Kingsley Amis and the right-wing tophilosopher Roger Scruton.

We weren't only opposed by the Tories and the Tory press. Mmany Labour politicians were appalled at us raising the issues of women's rights, racism and homophobia. Years later, the former Labour leader Roy Hattersley said, 'You have no idea how deeply offensive those issues were in my local working men's club.'

That September we honoured our promise to cut bus and Tube fares by 30 per cent, which became national news when the law lords ruled that cutting fares was illegal. This unleashed a massive and popular campaign, which eventually forced the law lords to allow us to cut fares two years later.

Oddly enough, Tony Benn's grandfather, John, had campaigned for cheap fares for working men when he was a member of the London County Council (LCC). Exactly in the same way as Peter Tatchell would be treated seventy-five years later, John Benn was the victim of a vile homophobic campaign by the *Sun*, which led to his defeat in the Bermondsey by-election.

After just a few weeks, two Labour members defected to the SDP, so our majority was cut to just four. But three Labour members were drinkers and one afternoon during the council meeting there was a tied vote. I noticed that our member Neil Davis wasn't in the chamber, but when I went to his office he was lying on the floor stinking of booze. I carried him back to the chamber just in time for the next vote and there was a lot of laughter as I had to hold his hand up because he wasn't conscious,

The Tories kept demanding, as they had the right to do, extra meetings, but given our tight majority I only allowed them to happen on Friday afternoons as three or four of the richer Tory members had always gone to their country homes and so we never lost a vote on Friday. Oddly enough the historian Suetonius, in his book *The Twelve Caesars*, recounts how Julius Caesar did the same thing when the reactionaries in the Roman Senate were trying to overthrow him.

Although we were depicted as Marxist revolutionaries, when I had a visit from the leader of the German Social Democrats, who spent the day discussing managing a major city, he ended up asking, 'Why do they call you such a radical?' An even more bizarre view came from an official at the Soviet Embassy, who told me they had been extremely worried by my election, as they feared I was a Trotskyist.

The *Time Out* journalist David Rose amazed me when he told me that there were now more files on me in Fleet Street than any other politician except for Margaret Thatcher. The radical left-wing Islington council leader Margaret Hodge came to complain to me that I was dominating the news so much that other councillors like her weren't getting any attention. I always thought it odd that the daughter of the millionaire steel magnate Hans Oppenheimer, who had gone to the private Bromley High School for Girls, had become the leader of the hard-left Labour caucus of the London boroughs. 'None of the boroughs can get any coverage,' she said. She wasn't amused when I said she only had to set up a lesbian and gay committee if she wanted coverage.

The right-wing Labour MP John Golding, who controlled Labour's National Executive Committee (NEC) was so appalled by me that he managed to rig the selection of the Labour candidate for Brent East to prevent me standing for Parliament in 1983. Out of 650 constituency Labour parties it was the only one that was not allowed to choose its own candidate.

As she announced her own 1983 election campaign, Thatcher included the promise to abolish the GLC even though the majority of her cabinet were opposed to the idea. Fortunately, letters between Thatcher and her local government minister Bernard Jenkins were leaked to us by a woman who ran a brothel. The papers had been taken out of the briefcase of one of her clients and we passed them on to the press. We continued to get letters when the same woman took her staff to the Tory conference in Blackpool, where this time the letters were taken from the briefcase while the owner was tied to the bed.

We never found out how it happened, but the police had been tipped off that we were getting access to cabinet papers. Bill Bush was driving to work one morning when he was forced to stop by Special Branch officers in an unmarked car, arrested and taken to the cells at Rochester Road police station. He was questioned for two hours before being allowed to make a phone call, and we immediately sent a lawyer to him and Tony Banks went to the House of Commons to raise the issue. Bernard Jenkins told the house he had no knowledge of what the police had done, but Labour MP Jack Straw jumped up to say, 'Before Thatcherism and its authoritarian tendencies became rampant there would not have been the climate in which the police could possibly have considered their powers to arrest and detain someone who worked for a leader of the Greater London Council.'

To challenge Thatcher's proposed abolition of the GLC, I resigned my seat and triggered a by-election, which would give voters the right to express their opinion about the abolition. Not only did the Tories refuse to contest the election, but this meant the only TV coverage I got was when my press officer managed to get me on to the breakfast TV programme, *Good Morning Britain*, with the fitness instructor Lizzie Webb. I had to wear a tracksuit while I bounced around as Mad Lizzie's exercise partner. My press officer also tried to get me a walk-on part in *EastEnders*, but the producers refused. I was quite annoyed when twenty-five years later Boris Johnson was allowed on as the Mayor of London.

One thing that really surprised me was getting a phone call from the Queen's staff saying she would like to open the Thames Barrier with me. As Thatcher was in the midst of her abolition campaign and would be furious about this, I was really amazed the Queen was prepared to annoy her. I was determined to be very careful about the event, because when the Tory GLC leader had got the press along to the nearly complete barrier just before the election, a steel cable had snapped and cut one of the workers on site in half. The TV crews filmed his body falling into the Thames but decided not to air it.

What really delighted me was that the Queen was happy to have my mum go with her on the boat down the Thames to the opening. I was waiting for them on site and as they all got off, Prince Philip said to me, 'Your mother's a lively old stick.' This was because Mum had spent the journey discussing which horses they were backing at the races that day. And when Prince Philip had asked Mum if she was warm enough, she replied, 'Oh yes, I've got a lot on underneath, dear.'

Following abolition it was only a year before the 1987 general election that would put me in Parliament. The Tories had selected a wonderful candidate, Harriet Crawley, a really nice thirty-nine-year-old moderate without a trace of racism or homophobia. Although she was single, the *News of the World* announced that she was pregnant, which prompted one woman on the street to ask her, 'Aren't you the one having Ken Livingstone's baby?'

CHAPTER NINE

From Parliament to the GLA

Although the world was gripped by the MPs expenses scandal in 2009, things were very different when I got elected to Parliament in 1987. You were only given enough of an allowance to employ one secretary and for months I had to wait to get a desk, so I was sitting in the corridors of the House of Commons answering my letters.

Although we were told about the pressure of all-night sittings in the House of Commons, the first time I encountered one of these it was just after midnight, when a Tory MP, Sir Nicholas Fairbairn, was completely drunk and rambled on for over twenty minutes. After he sat down, the equally drunk Labour MP Ron Brown got up and also rambled on. I decided this was a waste of time, so I went home for a quick nap and came back at 7.30 a.m. to find the debate was still going on. In the rest of my career as an MP I never once stayed overnight.

MPs who lived in London with their families were

usually keen to get home as soon as possible, but those who rented a flat because their family was living hundreds of miles away in their constituency ended up spending their nights drinking in the Commons bars. This led to a House of Commons peopled by two very different cultures.

I was immediately up to my neck in controversy when in my maiden speech I raised the allegation that rogue elements in MI5 had authorised the murder of the Irish Republic's most popular pop group, the Miami Showband, on 21 July 1975. I also revealed that the assassination squad was led by Robert Nairac, a captain in the British Army, who had previously crossed the border intending to murder a top IRA member, John Francis Green. A couple of years later, in May 1977, the IRA kidnapped Nairac and murdered him, so he had been venerated with a special plaque raised in his honour in the House of Commons. It took years for the truth to come out, but it was eventually revealed that the rogue element in MI5 had decided to murder the Miami Showband to bring to an end the ceasefire between Britain and the IRA. They did this because they feared if Harold Wilson's government negotiated a permanent solution, Wilson might be re-elected with a big majority, and these rogue elements in MI5 feared he was a Soviet agent. This covert MI5 operation was known as Clockwork Orange and I had to endure years of abuse until finally, in 1990, two civil servants found the only Clockwork Orange file that hadn't been destroyed as part of the cover-up.

Given that I only had enough money to employ one secretary, I couldn't have exposed all this without the help of a Brent East Labour-Party friend, Neil Grant, who was a teacher at the Jewish Free School. As soon as the school day was over Neil would come straight down to the House of Commons and helped draft 360 questions to the government about this covert murderous campaign. The journalist Paul Foot eventually published *Who Framed Colin Wallace?*, which exposed so much more and is still worth reading.

Labour leader Neil Kinnock did not put the government under any pressure about this scandal, but the terrorist group the Ulster Defence Association (UDA) decided I should be assassinated. The first I knew about this was when Special Branch officers turned up at my home unannounced one Saturday afternoon and told me that my movements were being monitored by extremist groups and I should change my pattern of travel. It was years later, when I was Mayor of London, that the press revealed that the UDA assassin had followed me, planning to shoot me as I walked down into Westminster Tube. Fortunately, MI5 had an undercover agent in the UDA leadership and talked them out of my being killed.

I had no chance of being given a position on Labour's front bench while Kinnock was leader, but lots of other activities started cropping up. The Dairy Council asked me to go on television to advertise red Leicester cheese alongside Ted Heath doing the same for blue Stilton. Birds Eye wanted me to advertise their potato waffles, but given the awful additives they contained, I said no. The BBC broadcast the spoof 'GLC: The Carnage Continues . . .' a *Comic Strip* episode in which Robbie Coltrane was portrayed as Charles Bronson playing me, with Jennifer Saunders portrayed as an alien monster masquerading as Thatcher. Kate

Bush sang the title track: 'Who's the man we all need? Ken! Who's the funky sex machine? Ken!'

All this media work stopped after Saddam Hussein invaded Kuwait in 1990, because companies couldn't have me advertising their goods while I was opposing our involvement in the invasion.

Two years later the next general election came along and, as I only had a majority of 1,653 votes, the Tories ran one of their strongest candidates against me, Damian Green, a devout Catholic opposed to abortion. As Brent East had the largest number of Catholic voters anywhere in England, the Society for the Protection of Unborn Children made me their number-one target and swamped the constituency with activists giving out leaflets with horrible pictures of aborted babies, warning that I was a leading pro-abortionist. Fortunately, Cardinal Hume turned up to open a homeless centre at the beginning of the campaign and praised my work. That went down very well with local voters and I had a landslide swing three times the national average.

With the war in Kuwait over, my media career bounced back and I appeared playing myself alongside Neil Pearson in Channel 4's *Drop the Dead Donkey*. This was followed by many appearances on *Have I Got News For You* and I also played myself in a miniseries called *A Woman's Guide to Adultery* alongside Amanda Donohoe and Theresa Russell. It took us twelve hours to record just four minutes of the programme and I was bored out of my skull but realised that actors certainly earned their money.

People would be surprised to know that I got on all right with Norman Tebbit because we both came from a working-class background, but as John Major's Tory government went into decline, he pinned me against a wall and asked: 'When are you going to get rid of this bloody awful government?'

Following New Labour's landslide in 1997, with Tony Blair's commitment to create a mayor for London, I watched with interest as Blair struggled to find a candidate. He'd asked Bob Ayling, CEO of British Airways, and Virgin's Richard Branson, but they weren't keen, given the very limited powers the mayor was going to be given. When my name came up, the Labour MP Gerald Kaufman said, 'I'd rather vote for Jeffrey Archer or even Saddam Hussein than Ken Livingstone.'

Fortunately, my media earnings meant I could employ another aide and took on board the very talented Simon Fletcher, who organised the Ken's Right to Stand campaign. Blair was now getting desperate and asked Mo Mowlam, the Labour MP for Redcar, to stand, but she told him, 'I'm not a Londoner and it's a shitty job.' Blair then asked celebrity chef Delia Smith, manager of Manchester United Alex Ferguson, independent MP Martin Bell and actress Joanna Lumley. The Tories were having a similar problem when both broadcaster Gyles Brandreth and former Tory MP David Mellor said no.

We called our first public meeting to support my campaign in a small room at Westminster Central Hall, but by the time I had turned up over a thousand people had arrived and we had to move up to the Great Hall. Beryl Bainbridge, Jo Brand and Mark Steele were all there to support me and Neil Pearson became the treasurer of my campaign. At the next meeting along came Arthur Smith, Kevin Day, Phill Jupitus and Billy Bragg.

Blair set out to rig the leadership ballot in favour of Frank Dobson (who knew nothing about the dodgy dealings). A third of all the votes were given to just fifty-seven London Labour MPs, which meant that each MP's vote was worth a thousand ordinary members' votes and 10,000 trade unionists' votes. A Labour press office representative told the *Independent*: 'We want to see Ken's blood on the carpet. This is the way to do it.'

Even with this appallingly rigged ballot I would still have won, but the South London Coop and two trade unions refused to allow their members to vote and just cast their votes for Frank. The members of the biggest union, the Transport and General Workers' Union (T & G), voted for me by 86 per cent to Glenda Jackson's 7 per cent and Frank's 7 per cent. Downing Street now got lots of old lefties lined up to denounce me, with Margaret Hodge writing an article deploring my incompetence. I ignored her rather than reminding people that when she was the leader of Islington Council, she chose to ignore allegations of child abuse in Islington's children's homes, which went on for many more years.

Fortunately, attention switched to the activities of the Tory mayoral candidate Jeffrey Archer, with stories that he had been having sex with his mistress, Sally Farmiloe, in a car park during a Tory ball in Mayfair. This did not stop Tory leader William Hague supporting him because of his 'probity and integrity'. Soon afterwards Archer had to withdraw after a friend who gave evidence in Archer's 1987 libel case against the *Daily Star* admitted he had lied and Archer went to prison for perjury. The Tories then turned to Seb Coe, Hague's chief of staff, who also said no, but finally they settled on Steve Norris, a former MP.

Just as the Labour selection campaign came to an end, New Labour banned three trade unions – which would all have overwhelmingly supported me – from taking part in the selection. It only came out after the campaign that several Labour MPs had been collecting ballot papers from their local members and destroying those who had voted for me. When the result was announced, 22,275 members had voted for Frank, with 74,646 voting for me, but the ballot rigging meant that Frank had won by 51.5 per cent to my 48.5 per cent.

I had no option but to stand as an independent for mayor, and won a convincing majority on 4 May 2000. The first words I said after the result was announced were, 'As I was saying, before I was so rudely interrupted fourteen years ago.' The *Daily Mail* warned: 'Left-wing extremist Ken Livingstone seizes control.' The *Daily Telegraph* said: 'Livingstone represents the Beckhamisation of politics.' The *Independent on Sunday* warned 'Ken has his eyes on Number Ten' and the *Sunday Telegraph* said I was not up to the job. *The Times* claimed that 'Putin is said to be an admirer'. Oddly enough, Margaret Thatcher came up to me at an event and said, 'Stick to your guns: everyone will be trying to tell you to do something else, but you must keep your resolve. You're now the leader of the equivalent of a small nation. Resolute, that's what you must be, resolute.' This struck me as a bit odd, given just fifteen years previously she was comparing me to a communist dictator, but the mood on the streets was amazing, with everyone shaking my hand and slapping me on the back. After the vote was analysed it turned out that I had got the support of 46 per cent of Labour voters, 33 per cent of Lib Dems and, bizarrely, 24 per cent of Tories.

As leader of the GLC I had been managing the forty-seven other Labour members, but the American mayoral system, which is used at City Hall, is completely different. You're the chief executive of the whole machine and every decision is made by you. Just ten days after the election I was completely knackered and woke up one morning to find my leg swollen. My GP thought it was thrombosis and whisked me off to hospital. Fortunately it turned out to be a Baker's cyst caused by my spending too long on my knees gardening.

One of the most important things was to clamp down on the way the bus companies were ripping London off. Back in my GLC days, Tube and bus drivers earned the same, but after bus privatisation bus drivers' wages had been slashed to just £16,000 a year, compared with the Tube drivers on £25,000. Having organised a wage increase for the bus drivers, I couldn't get on a bus without the driver congratulating me.

A lot of people were amazed when the person I appointed to run Transport for London was the American Bob Kiley, who had joined the CIA in 1963 and had ended up as exec-utive assistant to CIA director Richard Helms, who been given a suspended prison sentence for lying to Congress and covering up assassinations. But Bob and I hit it off immediately and I was delighted to discover that he had spent a lot of his time driving Robert Kennedy to election rallies in his campaign to be president in 1968.

Although everyone thought I wouldn't get on with the head of London's police, both Sir John Stevens and his deputy, Ian Blair, had a great working relationship with me. Towards the end of my first year in office, I was with Sir John at a police officers' annual dinner when he got word that there had been a fire in my office. Fearing this might be a deliberate attempt on my life, Sir John sent armed police to my home. Sitting in the car with Sir John, his protection officer asked me, 'Can you think of anybody who might have a grudge against you?' I laughed and said, 'How long have you got?'

About a year after I was elected mayor, my partner and I had an amiable separation and I started seeing other women. Fortunately, the *Evening Standard* was edited by Max Hastings, who was fair and honest, and the paper had just two paragraphs saying I had been seen on cosy dates with a Lib Dem. Sadly, the Lib Dems forced her to resign from her assembly seat and I never saw her again.

The gloomy media continued their usual dirty job with the *Daily Mirror* describing me as 'a petty man, a work-shy dullard, a bone-idle pedant'. The *Standard* under Max was more fair, saying I had made 'a bold start, we wish him well', but then he was replaced by Veronica Wadley as editor and she refused to meet me for the next five years and immediately started hysterical coverage about traffic problems in London. She claimed that the traffic speed was now only three miles per hour in central London because

I had given pedestrians two seconds longer to cross the road, saying 'motorists, this is your nightmare, an outdated lunacy'. I didn't know what had happened to my old friend Kate Hoey when she stood up in Parliament saying, 'What is the government going to do to stop Ken Livingstone's dictatorship?'

I had had similar rubbish as GLC leader when there were weeks of hysterical press coverage after I had introduced traffic lights at Hyde Park Corner. The papers never reported that accidents were cut by half.

All the media were focused on 17 February 2003, the day that the Congestion Charge would start. As I left home at six that morning, there were twenty TV cameras and a crowd of journalists waiting outside. As I walked to the Tube, I realised they were going to follow me all day because they believed the Congestion Charge would be a disaster and I would be forced to resign. But from the moment it started at 7 a.m., it worked perfectly and within a couple of hours all the journalists and TV crews had left. Traffic speeds returned to twelve miles per hour and there was a 20 per cent cut in carbon emissions and deadly nitrous oxide, and particulates went down by 12 per cent. The *Daily Telegraph* said, 'What if the wretched thing works after all?' although the *Sun* called it 'Ken's Big Con'. And Richard Littlejohn, a *Sun* columnist at the time, admitted the 'traffic is quicker, but the scheme was drawn up by a sexually inadequate, Lycra-clad, *Guardian*-reading, cycle-mad control freak'. Fortunately, the public didn't believe the papers and ten days later my poll ratings had gone up by 10 per cent. This was just at the time we were replacing

5,500 clapped-out old buses with 8,000 new ones, with more people now getting on the bus than in any time since the 1950s.

We were having similar successes with the police. When I became mayor there were only 25,000 but I eventually raised that figure to 35,000 including 630 neighbourhood police teams across London. Crime started falling all over the city.

I doubt if you need me to tell you much about our bid for the 2012 Olympics, but back then virtually no one thought we had a chance of winning, with my old Labour colleague Paul Boateng saying bidding for the Olympics 'would be madness'. I was working closely with the Labour minister Tessa Jowell and we got on fine. We appointed Barbara Cassani to prepare for our bid and I was able to get £2.9 billion more to upgrade our transport system so it could cope with a tidal wave of Olympic tourists.

I was still not a member of the Labour Party and it was reported in the press that Labour had approached MP Chris Smith, Channel 4 newsreader Jon Snow, police commissioner Brian Paddick and, bizarrely, even the former Tory candidate Steve Norris to run against me for mayor in 2004. The *Daily Mail* reported that nightclub owner Peter Stringfellow and the Egyptian businessman Mohamed al-Fayed, who wanted to scrap all bus lanes, were thinking of running as independents. As my poll ratings went up, Blair decided to bring me back in to the Party, and at the Labour leadership hearing, where I was questioned, John Prescott asked, 'Is there anything in your private life which could be damaging to the Party if it came out?' Everyone except

John laughed as I replied, 'Nothing the Party hasn't used against me already.'

Following my easy re-election as mayor, we started work on persuading the government to allow us to build Crossrail – a new underground line running from Heathrow through the City of London to the East End. It had been proposed in 1967 and would have cost just £300 million then. It would take me to the end of 2007 to get the government to agree, which I managed to do by taking Ed Balls, effectively deputy to Gordon Brown, out to dinner and explained that although we needed £5 billion from the government, it would generate another £10–15 billion in tax income for the government once it was built. At the end of the evening he promised to get it agreed, but warned it would take a few months. A couple of days later, City Hall's finance boss came to see me personally to query why my expenses claim for the dinner had two bottles of wine on the bill, given there was only me and Ed having the dinner. I pointed out that we had got £5 billion out of Ed and she begrudgingly accepted that this was just about acceptable for the price of an extra bottle of wine.

A lot of the press were starting to ramp up Islamophobia in the aftermath of the horrific bus and Tube bombings in 2005, but since my election in 2000 all racist, anti-Semitic and homophobic incidents recorded by the police had declined each year. Not long after the 2000 election I had been rude to a journalist who was chasing me down the street at nine at night. I had no idea he was Jewish, but I was denounced in Veronica Wadley's *Evening Standard* as anti-Semitic for having been rude to him. Bizarrely, a lot of the right-wing press challenged this. Andrew Alexander in the *Daily Mail* said, 'This issue has become one of freedom of speech. It does British Jewry's reputation no good to have the Deputies leading a campaign against free speech . . . which means the right to irritate, annoy, dismay and shock.' In the *Observer* Richard Ingrams wrote: 'When it comes to sensitivity to attack, there is no one so sensitive as a journalist . . . They make a living from heaping abuse and ridicule on those whom they do not approve . . . I urge Livingstone to stand firm.' Peter Hitchens in the *Mail on Sunday* said I was 'a cunning, nasty, narrow-minded, anti-British bigot, who has done more damage to this country than almost anyone living . . . But it was not racist. Nor was it anti-Semitic. Nor should he apologise for the incident.' In the *Daily Telegraph* Boris Johnson wrote, 'Ken, whatever you do, don't apologise . . . I speak as one who has been caught up in the modern mania for apology . . . It would be a surrender to media bullying . . . These words were not in themselves anti-Semitic.'

I knew that the 2008 mayoral election would be the most difficult because I had to increase fares to build the East London line, a new DLR line to Stratford International and to upgrade the North London line, and sadly none of these would open until just after the election. But our policies were having an effect and London overtook New York to be rated as the world's leading financial city, and although only a year had passed since the bombings, 2006 saw our highest level ever of tourists visiting the capital. My poll ratings were so good that the Tories couldn't find anyone to stand again. They talked about the DJs Mike Read and

Neil Fox, along with Jeremy Clarkson, Carol Thatcher and Sir Alan Sugar. Peter Stringfellow said he would like to be mayor 'but it does seem like four years of very hard work, so maybe I'll leave it to Ken Livingstone after all'.

Just under a year before the election Blair retired and Gordon Brown took over as prime minister. Finally, for the first time I was allowed to meet him at the laying of wreaths on the second anniversary of the Tube bombings. I took him to one side and quietly told him that the partial privatisation of the Underground that he had pushed through against my advice hadn't worked and the companies running it were £2 billion in debt and about to collapse. He told me to let his office know and we never talked about it again, but his government picked up the bill.

I couldn't believe how well things were going. London had now been listed as the first choice for foreign companies to come and we were getting the lion's share of foreign investment in Europe, with 388 projects coming in the year before the election.

Just five years previously the Lonely Planet guide had said that London was a 'joyless, decaying city where people are more likely to attack you than extend a welcome'. Now London was described as the best city in Europe 'enjoying a dramatic renaissance, sailing high on a wave of determination, optimism and glee'.

The Tories were still trying to find a candidate. John Major refused, so Tory party leader David Cameron asked the BBC boss Greg Dyke, which was a bit odd, given he had once been part of my GLC left-wing caucus. But Sir Digby Jones, CBI boss, also declined.

TV presenters Nick Ross and Anne Robinson were asked, but refused. Writing in the *Daily Telegraph*, Charles Moore called for a new Mayor of London whose 'first gesture of London's reconciliation with its national hinterland should be something which, for Ken Livingstone, is blasphemy, a St George's Day parade'. Clearly he hadn't bothered to check and find out that we had been celebrating St George's Day for years.

Just a few days before the close of nominations, Cameron persuaded Boris Johnson to stand. He was immediately supported by my old lefty colleague Kate Hoey, who said, 'Boris will do quite well. In theory I'm backing Mr Livingstone, but there's a feeling that the mayor is perhaps a kind of elected dictator.' The British Chamber of Commerce warned, 'Ken is a serious player and fights hard for London. Boris will have to rid himself of being seen as an eccentric figure if he is to have an impact.' The following Monday afternoon the media waited outside City Hall for Boris, who arrived late on his bike. He claimed he would put the smile back on London's face, but when asked what his policies would be, he just said, 'Wait and see.' Asked what I was doing wrong, he said, 'I'll get to you on that.' He then cycled off, not realising City Hall is circular and so he was surprised to run into the journalists again.

Boris had been a wild cheerleader for the Iraq war, saying, 'To stand in Baghdad and look at the contrast between the Americans ... and Iraqis, skinny and dark, badly dressed and fed.' His policy statements were equally bizarre. He ignored the fact that house building in London had increased from 17,000 a year in 2000 to 27,000 and promised to abolish my rule that half of new homes should be affordable housing. Ignoring the 50 per cent increase in bus users, he promised to scrap the mayor's powers to regulate buses and introduce full privatisation of the bus service.

Sadly, Boris had become a regular guest on *Have I Got News For You*, which boosted his popularity, as he always made everybody laugh at his outrageous comments. Nowadays, being witty on a TV sofa does more to boost your standing than a serious talk about policy. Polls showed that over 80 per cent of voters recognised Boris.

At the 2007 Tory conference Boris spoke over a live satellite link to Arnold Schwarzenegger, Governor of California, who kept rolling his eyes during Boris's speech, saying, 'He's fumbling all over the place.' Mayor of New York Michael Bloomberg said, 'Perhaps the acoustics were bad or my hearing's not what it was. Or perhaps Boris was talking rubbish.'

Boris kept promising to cut crime in London but never mentioned that as I started increasing police numbers, it fell by 2.2 per cent in 2003, 4.3 per cent in 2004–5 and 4.4 per cent in 2006. We were on the verge of a 25 per cent cut in crime since the beginning of the decade. Murders were down from 222 in 2003 to 160 in 2007. Rape and gun crime had been cut by a quarter each.

At the *Spectator* awards, just six months before the election, Veronica Wadley told Boris, 'You've got to pull your finger out,' and the *Daily Telegraph*'s Peter Oborne wrote: 'Cameron is tearing his hair out at Boris's lazy campaign.' George Osborne, Shadow Chancellor of the Exchequer, gave Boris a dressing-down because of his invisibility due to a heavy filming schedule with the BBC. At the Jewish Forum when he was asked what he liked about London, Boris replied, 'You can go into Tesco and buy mange tout or at your newsagent get mango juice.'

After the first candidates' debate on ITV, the *Morning Star* reported Boris's unfamiliarity with the issues, but the *Evening Standard* disagreed, saying that Boris had clearly won and that I 'appeared an angry old man from a bygone era; dressed in grey, he looked tired and every one of his sixty-two years. He became angry very quickly.'

In February, the *Times* said I was spending £75 million on our bike-hire scheme, which would have 6,000 bikes by the summer of 2010 and then double in numbers. Plans for twelve cycle superhighways were reported in the *Guardian* (but after the election Boris cancelled these). My plan was to increase cycling in London by 400 per cent. When Boris won, he dropped my plan and went for an even more expensive bike-hire scheme, which cost £12,000 for each bike and docking frame and pushed the cost up to £80 million.

Bizarrely, Prince Charles decided to intervene in the election in a speech claiming that tall buildings pockmarked the city. The *Telegraph* was delighted at this 'thinly veiled attack on the policies of Ken Livingstone'. Madonna told *The Times*, 'Now all Red Ken wants is roadworks going on everywhere. I would make it so that aspiring musicians wouldn't have to pay the Congestion Charge or pay taxes. They should be exempt.' Chef Gordon Ramsay called for me to be dropped in the Thames. The *Evening*

Standard claimed the cost of the Olympics would double and that 'Suicide bomber backer runs Ken's campaign'. The *Standard* also claimed that one of my TFL board members, Dabinderjit Singh, was linked to a banned terrorist group and also to a plane bomb that had killed 329 people in 1985. The truth was that Singh was a chief auditor at the Ministry of Defence and had the second-highest security clearance possible.

Tragically, the British economy had slipped into recession, and just weeks before polling day the 10p tax band was abolished, which hit the poorest hardest, with those earning less than £18,000 seeing their tax double. My canvassers said this was playing badly on the doorstep, and Labour's pollster, Philip Gould, said 'after the March budget Labour's vote and yours just went off a cliff'. Boris now had a twelve-point lead. At the end of polling day I was so exhausted, I fell asleep before the results came in from councils outside London, but when I turned on the radio at 7 a.m. and heard the Tories had 44 per cent nationally to Labour's 24 per cent, I knew I needed to go in to City Hall and pack up my things. That night as we waited to go on stage for the result, Boris said, 'This is not you, it's Brown's fault.' Boris had won by 6 per cent.

Tears rolled down my cheeks as my older kids phoned to commiserate, and I spent the weekend with all the kids. On the following Tuesday my teammates came over with their analysis of how the voting had gone and I was proud of the fact that I had run ahead of the Labour Party in all London's 630 wards, inner and outer, rich or poor, black or white, Muslim or Jewish.

At City Hall Boris was telling the staff he was not a 'crazed neo-Con' and that 'the differences between me and the previous mayor have been greatly exaggerated'. But as the transport schemes I had started were completed, I was never invited to the opening of any of them. Boris cancelled our deal with Venezuela, which meant we lost £56 million, and he sacked the staff running my environmental schemes and cancelled them.

Prince Charles sent Boris a handwritten letter of 'warm regards' with proposals for what he should do on planning issues. When Boris was being briefed on the crime figures he joked 'the biggest crime is that I got elected on a platform of cutting crime when crime rates were already going down under Ken'. He laughed, but was embarrassed when nobody else did.

Undoubtedly, the *Evening Standard*'s vicious and dishonest campaign against me under the editorship of Wadley had done damage, but it had also damaged her paper, as the sales fell from 425,000 to just 160,000 a day.

One good thing was that after Boris said he wasn't going to attend the Beijing Olympics in 2008, the Mayor of Beijing had me flown out for the opening ceremony instead. Although I had never really been into sport, I'm never going to forget the elation I felt in 2005 when it was announced in Singapore, where all the delegate cities were gathered, that the UK had won the Olympic bid. My staff had worked extremely hard on the campaign and when the news came through that London had won, they rang to congratulate me from City Hall, very excited. I found out later that everyone in the city was celebrating and it was an overwhelming feeling of pure joy that London was successful and united in celebrating something so positive.

Losing to Boris brought my eight years as mayor to an end, but looking back over my working life, they were the best eight years I had ever experienced. When I was leader of the GLC I was managing my Labour group, but as mayor I could take a decision almost instantaneously and that was it. If I look at what I did, not just to win the Olympics, but to transform our transport system, I'm proud of that legacy. When I became mayor I was told London was failing and firms were thinking of leaving, but I turned it round and Boris inherited the most dramatically booming city in Europe. Sadly, Boris just spent the next eight years promoting himself and the new mayor Sadiq Khan inherited a city with many problems, which was Boris's legacy. It's always going to be difficult to have a fair election when most of our papers are in the hands of right-wing editors and owners, but every four years Londoners need to ensure that they elect someone who loves this city and is going to work to improve it.

No one in London will ever forget their fear and their emotions when on 7 July 2005 four terrorists let off bombs: three on underground trains and one on a bus, killing fifty-two people. They had all been born and raised in Britain but not in London and were protesting against Tony Blair's invasion of Iraq. Their plan was obvious: they wanted to divide London, andthey wanted to see attacks on London's Muslims which they believed would fuel a counter-wave of attacks by Muslims against other Londoners.

In my speech, after thanking the firefighters and police, I said:

'I want to say one thing specifically to the world today. This was not a terrorist attack against the mighty and the powerful. It was not aimed a presidents or prime ministers. It was aimed at ordinary, working-class Londoners – black and white, Muslim and Christian, Hindu and Jew, young and old. It was an indiscriminate attempt to slaughter, irrespective of any considerations for age, for caste, for religion. That isn't an ideology, it isn't even a perverted faith, it is just an indiscriminate attempt at mass murder – and we know what the objective is. They seek to divide Londoners. They seek to turn Londoners against each other. I said yesterday to the International Olympic Committee that the city of London is the greatest in the world because everybody lives side by side in harmony; Londoners will not be divided by this cowardly attack. They will stand together in solidarity alongside those who have been injured and those who have been bereaved and this is why I am proud to be the mayor of that city.

Finally, I wish to speak through you directly to those who came to London today to take life. I know that you personally do not fear to give your own life in exchange for taking others – that is why you are so dangerous. But I know you do fear you may fail in your long-term objective to destroy our free society, and I can show you why you will fail. In the days that follow look at our airports, look at our seaports and look at our railway stations, and even after your cowardly attack, you will see that people from the rest of Britain, people from around the world will arrive in London to become Londoners and to fulfil their dreams and achieve their potential. They chose to come to London, as so many have come before because they come to be free, they come to live the life they choose, they come to be able to be themselves. They flee you because you tell them how they should live. They don't want that and nothing you do, however many of us you kill, will stop that flight to our cities where freedom is strong and where people can live in harmony with one another. Whatever you do, however many you kill, you will fail.'

But Londoners weren't going to be divided, and stood together and in the days that followed the police did not record a single incident of an attack of any form on any Muslim or Muslim institution. I don't think there was ever a moment when I was so proud to be a Londoner as in those days. Even more remarkable was the fact that in the following year tourists coming to London increased, which none of us could ever believe would happen.

There is a long history of terrorism in London. Back in the reign of Queen Victoria our politics were torn apart by the demands of the Irish Fenians for the right to Home Rule by the Irish. In December 1867, a Fenian bomb went off at Clerkenwell Green, killing twelve The bomber, Michael Barrett, was caught, convicted and was the last person to be publicly hanged in Britain. Three more bombs were set off in 1883, one on a Metropolitan Line train at Praed Street, injuring sixty-two people, followed the next year by four more attacks, with two injured at Victoria station.

Terrorism was renewed in London in 1971 when the IRA set off a bomb at the Post Office Tower and in the years that followed others were let off at Earls Court Boat Show, Madame Tussauds, the Tower of London (where one woman died), Tottenham Court Road, Soho, Chelsea (with one dead), Selfridges (with five injured) and Harrods. In 1975 bombs went off at Woodford, Oxford Street and in Kensington an officer died trying to defuse the bomb that had been discovered. Two more died in a bomb explosion at the Hilton Hotel. In 1979 the Tory MP closest to Mrs Thatcher, Airey Neave, died when his car exploded.

Just after I had become GLC leader in 1981, two died and forty were injured when a bomb exploded at Chelsea Barracks. One was badly injured in a car bomb in Dulwich, one died in Oxford Street and fortunately, the bomb at Debenhams was disarmed. The following year two died and twenty-three were injured in Hyde Park, and six died and thirty were injured in Regent's Park. Just before Christmas that year, six died and ninety were injured as a bomb went off at Harrods.

I was viciously denounced in the Tory press for saying we had to negotiate with the IRA in order to bring this bombing to an end, but Thatcher relentlessly refused ever to negotiate, claiming that this had nothing to do with politics and these were merely 'criminals and psychopaths'. When I first invited Sinn Fein leader Gerry Adams to come to London, Thatcher banned him from entering England, so I flew out to Belfast to meet him. Virtually the first thing he told me was that the IRA knew they could never defeat the British Army, but the British Army could never defeat the IRA: there had to be negotiations. Tragically, over another thousand people would die until Tony Blair finally negotiated a peace deal with the IRA following his election in 1997.

But it was never just the IRA doing the bombing. In 1999 fifty were injured by a nail bomb in Brixton and the following week six were injured by a nail bomb in Brick Lane. And then the Lord Admiral Duncan, a gay pub in Old Compton Street, saw three killed and many injured. Clearly a man targeting black, Asian and gay people was bound to be from the far right and eventually David Copeland was arrested and convicted of these crimes.

CHAPTER TEN

Transport

B ack in 1872 Gustave Doré painted a picture of the traffic jam of horse-drawn carts, Hackney cabs and buses
and even sheep stuck in the road at Ludgate Circus. From
1850 London had been caught in traffic gridlock. Maps
from the time show that London really only extended as far
as what we would call inner London today – north of the
river, barely half of Lambeth, Southwark and Lewisham,
and nothing west of Hammersmith or east of the docks.
All train stations were at the edge of the city and it was
only in 1863 that the first underground train (in the world)
left Paddington station to travel three-and-a-half miles to
Euston, King's Cross and eventually on to Farringdon. It
was a steam locomotive, so before long there were problems
with pollution in the tunnel. By the turn of the century,
seven lines had been completed, with 800 trains a day
scheduled.'

London had gone from 1 million citizens in 1800 to 2.5

million by 1851, making it the largest city in the world. By 1911 there were over 7 million Londoners (more than Paris, Moscow, Berlin and St Petersburg together). But the grid-lock was showing that any further increase in population would have to rely on a big expansion of the Underground. By 1879 you could get what is now the Jubilee line from Swiss Cottage to Willesden Green, and the following year to Harrow, and twelve years later to Aylesbury. But there was still the problem with the pollution in the underground tunnels. It was only in 1890 that the first electric Tube train ran from Stockwell to the City in a sixty-foot-deep tunnel, taking just eighteen minutes and carrying 15,000 passengers a day. Over the next ten years, five more Tube lines were agreed by the House of Commons with the Central line from Shepherd's Bush to Bank and Liverpool Street seeing building works start in 1896. The construction of the Bakerloo line began in 1898, but the firm went bankrupt and work was suspended. The owner of the firm, James Whitaker Wright, was put on trial for stealing £5 million from his investors. Having been found guilty, as he was led out of the court he swallowed a cyanide pill and killed himself.

Fortunately he was replaced by Charles Yerkes who came from Chicago to take over the District line in 1901 and introduced the electric conductor rail system, extending the line to East Ham, Hounslow, Harrow, Ealing, Richmond and Wimbledon.

The Bakerloo, Northern and Piccadilly lines were taken over by Yerkes's successor (he died in 1905) and were completed by 1906. Although there were several extensions into the suburbs, no new Tube line would be built through London for sixty-two years, when we finally got the Victoria line in 1968. The Victoria line now seems so small and packed out with people, but the decision to build it was made when the government still had the plan to reduce London's population to just 5.5 million by 1990, and so they thought they were building a new Tube line for a smaller London.

By 1908 the Tube as we know it today was largely all in place. Albert Stanley became the boss of the Underground group in 1910 and the first chair of London Transport – called the London Passenger Transport Board (LPTB) at the time – in 1933. He made Frank Pick the chief executive of LPTB in 1933 after Pick had spent twenty-seven years working on underground projects. They worked together for over thirty years. Pick is most famous for designing the Underground map.

After the First World War, Tube extensions into the suburbs so we could build 'homes fit for heroes' led to twenty years of the fastest growth in our history. In 1926 the Northern line ran from Edgware to Malden and two years later Piccadilly station was reconstructed with eleven escalators because it had gone from 1.5 million passengers in 1907 to 18 million a year in 1922. With the expansion, Piccadilly station could handle 50 million passengers per year. The impact of the expansion of the Tube is most clear when you look at examples like the transformation of farmland at Golders Green into a new town once the Tube station opened. Altogether, between 1918 and 1939 860,000 new homes were built in London – 43,000 a year.

After the Second World War the government agreed to an extension of the Central line, but after that concentrated on investment in British Rail and neglected the Underground. In 1953 the government was investing £5.9 million a year in the road system and a mere £300,000 in the Tube. So we had to wait until 1962 for a government to agree to build the Victoria line.

All governments were becoming obsessed by cars. London went from just under half a million cars in 1950 to 2 million fifteen years later. And in 1963 Lord Beeching produced his ghastly report recommending the closure of one third of the British Rail network.

London's politics in the early 1970s became dominated by government plans to build three massive ring roads. It was still the thinking that one day everyone would have a car and slowly public transport would fade away. But the simple truth is unless you want to build a city like Los Angeles, where half of all the land is covered by roads, motorways and car parks, that just wouldn't work, and the impact on the environment would be deadly.

Back in 1977 there was a plan to extend the Archway Road north, wrecking many hundreds of homes and ruining the environment, so I got involved in the campaign to stop it, turning up day after day at the public inquiry to protest. At one point the protestors got so raucous that the chairman of the inquiry was scared enough to climb out onto the roof to escape. I followed him out, as the only way off the roof was to jump to your death. I was trying to persuade him to come back in when the barrister leading the case for the motorway followed me out onto the roof screaming, 'Don't push him off!' The barrister went on to become the leader of the Tory Party – Michael Howard.

Public opposition to the ring roads led to the Labour GLC administration that was elected in 1973 cancelling the project and reversing the policy that London's population should be reduced to just 5.5 million by 1990. We had to stop London from declining.

The lack of investment in the Underground meant that Tube journeys dropped from 720 million a year in 1948 to just 498 million by 1982. Now it has risen to over 1.25 billion. Another factor in putting people off the Underground may well have been the horror of the Moorgate crash on the last day in February 1975, when the driver of a packed Tube train drove it straight into the wall at the end of the tunnel, killing over forty passengers and injuring dozens more. Still today no one knows why he did it.

In 1981, when I became leader of the GLC, we cut bus and Tube fares by 30 per cent and the number of Tube journeys went up by 10 per cent from day one. We also planned the modernisation of 140 Tube stations. Cutting fares and building council housing was hardly a Marxist agenda, but on the day I became leader, Thatcher made a speech to the Scottish Conservatives saying my plan was to turn Britain into a 'communist tyranny like those of Eastern Europe'. It wasn't just Thatcher who was scared that we were too radical, as was shown when Law Lords issued a bizarre judgement that ruled that cutting fares was illegal, even though back in 1969 Thatcher had stated that was what the legislation which passed control of transport to the GLC would have allowed us to do. Sadly, Thatcher's government was totally hostile to our fares cut and removed control of London Transport from us in 1984, just two years before she abolished the council.

No one anticipated the impact it was going to have on public transport at the time but in 1986 Thatcher triggered the 2008 financial crisis by deregulating our banking and financial system. Immediately bankers and financiers from around the world flooded into London because they were free to do things here that it was illegal to do back in their own countries. This vast increase in bankers meant the construction of new buildings, such as at Canary Wharf, and London's population began to grow again. Initially the government merely agreed to have a new light rail system to Canary Wharf, but by 1992 John Major's government realised that the city wasn't going to work without the construction of the Jubilee line.

By the time I became mayor in 2000, businesses were threatening to leave London because the chaos caused by gridlock and congestion meant the average speed of a car in central London was just nine-and-a-half miles an hour. The buses were even slower, with just 5,500 clapped-out old buses. When the Tories privatised the buses the new owners got rid of conductors so everyone getting on the bus had to buy a ticket from the driver, which meant you could wait three or four minutes at each bus stop before the bus could move on again. Building a Tube line takes decades and needs government permission, so to tackle London's congestion urgently it had to be the buses that were the answer to the problem. I took back control of the buses: freezing the fares, replacing the old buses by buying

8,000 new ones and putting in bus lanes so the buses could avoid traffic congestion. We also introduced Oyster cards to save time.

The most controversial thing I did, however, was the Congestion Charge. The city of Singapore had introduced a congestion charge back in 1970 but, except for one small Norwegian town, no other city had dared to take the risk. It took over two years to install all the cameras around the zone and during that time 98 per cent of all newspaper stories about the Congestion Charge predicted it would be a disaster. However, it worked perfectly from the first few moments, and traffic speeds went up to twelve-and-a-half miles an hour. The Americans didn't like my policy and the US Embassy refused ever to pay, with the result that over the years we have issued them with 45,000 fines, and they still owe £5 million. Japan ranks as the second-worst embassy, owing £3.5 million.

CHAPTER ELEVEN

Buildings: County Hall and the Houses of Parliament

Three buildings have had a major impact on my life. As a child the most overwhelming was the Natural History Museum. Built at the height of the glory of Victoria's empire, it was clearly designed to be the most amazing museum on the face of the planet, with the most extensive collection of animals on display anywhere in the world. As soon as my parents thought I was old enough to travel around London on my own, I kept going up to the Natural History Museum and exploring it bit by bit. As I walked in the front door, every time I was in awe of the great dinosaur hanging from the roof. Sadly, it has now been replaced by a whale.

The Tories had won control of the LCC for the first time in 1907, just as the council had decided to move to a new headquarters. With the Tories in charge, they inevitably wanted what was going to be a wonderful building for the councillors and a major extension into the Thames on the South Bank just north of Westminster Bridge was the chosen site. The building would take until 1933 before it was completed, with twelve miles of corridors covering five acres of land. It was only when I was elected to the GLC in 1973 that I entered County Hall for the first time, and I was overwhelmed. Seven thousand staff worked there in 1,200 rooms covering 1.2 million square feet. Walking up the grand staircase to the council chamber, you could look all the way along the 670-foot corridor that contained members' offices and was lined with wonderful imported oak, Portland stone and Italian marble. It was so long that on foggy days enough fog would leak in so that you couldn't see the end of the corridor. A great oval council chamber with 'ayes' and 'noes' lobbies on either side had been built and the chair in which the chairman presided over the meetings had been made from a petrified oak tree found at the bottom of the Thames when County Hall was being built. The Westminster Bridge Road entrance had its own courtyard where members parked their cars, but the public were not allowed in. There was a fantastic members' library, members' restaurant and, unlike MPs, every member had their own office or shared one. As a working-class boy from south London I couldn't believe the building I was in and wanted to spend the rest of my working life there.

Some of the Tories were very rich, like Willie Bell, who owned several buildings in Manhattan and Lena Townsend, who had been the Conservative leader of the Inner London Education Authority and had grown up on a houseboat on the River Nile. There was also a second houseboat for the family's horses. Although she was pleasant, she was worryingly eccentric about and suspicious of gay men, believing that any man wearing suede shoes was gay. In the three years she chaired the committee appointing head teachers, no teacher wearing suede shoes got the job.

The GLC was so busy doing so many things that virtually everybody was given a job and I was made vice-chair of the Film Viewing Board, so I was being paid £10 to watch each film that the film industry's panel had declined to give a certificate to. We had the power to overturn those decisions, but the bad thing about the job was that most of the appeals came from not-very-good films (many of them porn). The Film Viewing Board was the largest committee on the council and what was then seen as unpleasant porn is quite mild compared with what we now get to see after 9 o'clock on the telly. Forty-four years on, the only film I can vividly remember was a French one called *Blow-Out* which had been denied a permit on the grounds that it showed a prostitute masturbating on the exhaust of a Bugatti car. When the debate started after the film ended, nobody mentioned masturbation because two female Tory councillors from Bromley wanted it banned because there had been too much flatulence. I pointed out that the rules were that we could block a film because of violence or porn, but no one had ever banned a film because of farting.

In the run-up to the 1992 election the Tories expected Labour to win and one of Neil Kinnock's policies was to bring back a Greater London Council (GLC), to be housed in the then empty County Hall. Michael Portillo, who was the minister responsible for the building, dreaded the idea that there might be another lefty council putting up radical banners that could be seen from the House of Commons, so he sold it off. Even though the building had been given an estimated value of £250 million at the time of abolition, Portillo sold it for just £50 million, although the London School of Economics (LSE) had offered to buy it for more. Perhaps Portillo was worried that if it was owned by the LSE they might be prepared to hire a chunk of it out for a new London authority.

County Hall is now a hotel with the wonderful London Aquarium in its basement. I was taken to lunch at the hotel's restaurant a few years ago by a journalist, and I was struck by how much better the food now was.

One of the most impressive buildings in the world is undoubtedly the Houses of Parliament. because they were originally constructed as a royal palace rather than a Parliament. The high-vaulted ceilings and elaborately tiled floors look more like a grand church than a seat of government and this is because some areas were built so long ago under Edward the Confessor, with the rest being built in the Gothic Revival style popular in the mid-nineteenth century. When I was elected as an MP in 1987 I couldn't believe how dysfunctional this building was for a Parliament. There weren't enough offices for each MP to have somewhere to work (unlike County Hall) and I spent months using a corridor as my office. As I wandered around it always felt that I was in a great abbey, with the carvings of all our four nations' patron saints glaring down at me, and statues of many long-dead politicians.

Back in 1834 a great fire destroyed everything except the medieval Great Hall but instead of building a more modern new home for Parliament, the government of the day just rebuilt it exactly as it had been. Still today it is defined by the Royal Entrance, the Royal Staircase, the Royal Gallery and the Prince's Chamber. Although there have been over 600 MPs for centuries, the rebuilt chamber could only seat 420. The Commons chamber was burned to the ground once again during the Second World War and once again the government decided to rebuild it as it was, even though one or two MPs argued for a larger chamber and one that was circular in order to avoid the endless braying and shouting across the floor that dominates Prime Minister's Questions every week. When I was there, although there were not enough offices, there were so many bars and restaurants that I don't think I ever managed to eat and drink in all of them. To keep MPs happy, alcohol was sold to us at the wholesale price, meaning you could get a bottle of wine for £10 that would have cost £30 in a London restaurant.

It wasn't just the building that looked medieval – the messengers had to wear tailcoats and white ties as they carried notes from the members of the public who wanted to meet their MPs. In my days without an office, the only thing that I had access to was my reserved coat hook in the members' cloakroom and a locker. When I asked why there was a pink ribbon on each of the members' coat hooks, a police officer said it was for MPs to hang their swords on.

The most significant thing about that 1987 election was for the first time in history Londoners had elected three black MPs: Diane Abbott, Bernie Grant and Paul Boateng, but after a couple of days Bernie told me that as he tried to walk in up the members' staircase the police had stopped him, saying this was only for members of Parliament, and he took great pleasure in pointing out he was one.

Fortunately, in the 1990s the Metropolitan Police moved from old Scotland Yard to their new building in Victoria and suddenly I got my first office in the building they had vacated, as it was taken over by Parliament.

CHAPTER TWELVE

Food

One of the biggest shocks in my political career came in September 1989 when I lost my seat on Labour's National Executive Committee. Over the next three years Dennis Skinner and Tony Benn were also voted off. I think the reason the left was ousted was that after three election victories by Margaret Thatcher the membership fell in line with Neil Kinnock's view that we had to move to the right to have any chance of winning the next election.

With the left no longer seen as on the verge of power, I started to get all sorts of work from the media, with the BBC putting me on to chair a radio quiz programme (which I wasn't very good at). I was also often booked on *Have I Got News For You* and Michael Parkinson's weekly radio show on LBC with the Lib Dem MP Charles Kennedy and the funny Tory Jerry Hayes. But the biggest surprise came when Rosie Boycott, the editor of *Esquire* magazine, asked to see me. Twenty years earlier she'd first come to my attention as one of the leading feminists, co-editing *Spare Rib*. I assumed she wanted me to do a political column and almost fell over when she said she wanted me to be *Esquire*'s restaurant critic. I told her that although I loved food, I was no expert on either food or wine. But Rosie didn't mind that – as she said, 'Our readers are mainly white men from the south east with more money than sense who just want to know where to go for a good meal.'

I couldn't believe my luck, as I was now able to go to the most expensive restaurants, taking a friend along, with the bill being picked up by Rosie. But she had one firm rule, which was that I should never accept a free meal by the restaurant. Oddly enough, in the hundreds of restaurants I visited over the next three years, the only place that ever happened was in Harrods, where I had taken Mum for lunch. 'It's up to you whether you pay this or not, sir,' said the waiter. Mum couldn't believe that I insisted on paying.

While the rich drive expensive cars, go to exclusive restaurants, drink champagne and party through the night, no one expects to see lefties like me trundling around very expensive restaurants. For many people, the image of the left is one of rather dour misery, spending all our time on picket lines or handing out leaflets. My *Esquire* column gave me the chance to convince people that socialism and the good life are not incompatible.

I started at El Parador, an amazing Spanish restaurant in Eversholt Street, just round the corner from Mornington Crescent Tube. My three guests and I ordered four tapas dishes each to share, including a delicious squid cooked in ink and a marinated octopus that just dissolved in my mouth. We were all so bloated, but I was the only one still able to have a dessert: a delicious mousse with brandy. I kept going back to El Parador, introducing a lot of my leftie friends to it, who in turn spread the word. Sadly, the restaurant closed in the summer of 2018.

My next stop was at the Red Fort in Soho. Thirteen years previously I had been involved in a huge row on the Labour-controlled Camden Council over whether or not we should give a grant to Amin Ali and a few young Bengali waiters who wanted to set up the Red Fort as a cooperative restaurant. I never understood why the right-wingers were opposed to this, as it rapidly became one of London's best Indian restaurants and spawned four spin-offs.

Amin Ali remained very innovative. Unlike a lot of restaurants that just carry on producing the same meals, Amin would occasionally do a complete relaunch, including a food festival for which some of the greatest Indian chefs were flown in to London to invent new dishes. I had a wonderful spicy broth cooked with pulses, rice and mutton and garnished with coriander, followed by a fish called boal caught in a Bangladeshi river.

My third restaurant choice was Vasco & Piero's Pavilion in Poland Street. This was ten years after I had first met Clement Freud, a Liberal MP at the time, when we were both having lunch separately with female friends in the South Bank's Archduke wine bar. That same evening I had taken another friend to the Pavilion and was amazed to discover Clement was also there and also with a different woman from the one in the wine bar. Given the odds of this happening, my friend and I speculated that he might be working for MI5, monitoring restaurants serving dangerous lefties. As he got up, he came over and said, 'Where are you having breakfast?'

Clement told me that the Pavilion was his favourite restaurant. I had only discovered it by accident. For years I had gone to the Academy cinema in Oxford Street, which used to put on lots of left-wing European films, probably the reason it eventually closed. One evening in the middle of a film I got up to go for a wee but then took the wrong turning coming back to my seat and stumbled on the Pavilion, which was in the same building as the cinema. The Pavilion was one of the first restaurants to open after the Second World War and had employed an imaginative architect, who had designed it as an integral part of the cinema, with blue and gold art deco design. The food was also unique. The Italian wine list had some of the most delicious wines available, the pasta was always fresh, and they would create an on-the-spot new meal for any vegetarians who turned up.

When the cinema closed, the owners, Vasco and Piero, opened their restaurant just around the corner in Poland Street. For my review I had the sautéed oyster mushrooms with garlic and parsley on a bed of rocket, which was wonderfully rich but not filling, so I could cope with the grilled salmon that followed. Instead of my usual bottle of Gavi I tried the Borgo Conventi, an amazing honeyed Chardonnay. If you go, make sure you order their tiramisu, which is the best I have ever had. Thirty-five years on I am still going to the Pavilion and now take my five kids and their partners for our regular meals out.

While I was doing Michael's Parkinson's LBC radio slot with Charles Kennedy, I developed a real liking for Charles and so at the end of one programme I took him off to Grumbles in Churton Street, SW1. Apart from the Lib Dem leader Paddy Ashdown and the enormous Cyril Smith, Charles Kennedy was about the only Lib Dem MP anyone had heard of. He stunned everyone by getting elected in 1983 at the age of just twenty-three, making him the youngest MP in the Commons. Now at the age of thirty-three he was the most eligible bachelor with his bright red hair and huge sense of fun. I couldn't help pulling his leg and telling him he needed to settle down with someone soon or he'd be depicted as a confirmed bachelor: an altogether different kind of animal. He then told me he had just fallen in love, but made me promise not to give details about this in my restaurant column. He lived just round the corner and Grumbles was his favourite restaurant. I immediately saw why. It is a lovely, quiet and romantic place and with very reasonable prices. We both enjoyed the avocado and watercress salad and then a main course of Pacific prawns peri peri.

I was interested to know why Charles had chosen, in 1981, to join the Social Democratic Party (the SDP, which merged with the Liberal Party in 1988) rather than the Liberals, because back in those days the Liberals were much more fun. I really enjoyed telling him about the senior GLC officer who had been a lifelong Liberal but could no longer face going to the Liberal conferences because he couldn't stand the sandal-wearing, bearded, wholefood freaks trying to get him into bed. Charles roared with laughter, pointing out that nothing like that ever happened at an SDP conference.

After almost a year as a restaurant critic I felt it was time to write about the quality of the food in the House of Commons. Members of the public cannot get in except at the invitation of an MP, but you'll be pleased to know that only an MP is allowed to pay the bill. The restaurants in the mother of parliaments are like Britain's Ancien Régime, reflecting our rigid class system, starting with the policeman's caff at the bottom of the pile and working your way up to the Churchill Room, which is reserved for the toffs. Parliament's food improved during my time as an MP, with a real growth of vegetarian offers. Thirty years before that, the food was pretty basic but the wine cellar was one of the best in Europe. For several hundred years the chair of the catering committee (always a Tory) toured French vineyards and ordered the best wines for the House of Commons. Tragically this all came to an end in 1964 when Robert Maxwell, the disgraced millionaire news magnate, became an MP and chair of the catering committee. Having taken one look around the cellar, he decided it was too good to be wasted on common MPs and sold the entire collection of wine to himself. Not surprisingly, records of the sale were destroyed in a fire. I first met Maxwell in1985 and he was still drinking his way through the legacy of the House of Commons wine cellar.

The best restaurant in the House is the Members' Dining Room, which is only open to MPs and therefore this is where all the plotting and rumour mongering takes place. As well as the food being heavily subsidised, you can pick up all the latest news about which cabinet members are having sex with each other. Another great restaurant is the Churchill Room; however, it isn't the food that is striking but the artwork commemorating our great wartime leader, with many of his own paintings on the walls and several portraits of him in between. Fortunately, no one dared to suggest creating a Thatcher Room to commemorate the Falklands War.

One of the problems with our Parliament is it has so many members it's about the largest in the world. When I was elected there were 271 Labour MPs, far too many to get to know well. I saw MPs in two categories: not left or right or even Labour or Tory, but those who would talk to me and those who would rush past, staring straight ahead. Oddly enough, Tony Blair was in the talker camp and always chatted to me, but I could never get him to talk about the deal he struck with Gordon Brown that persuaded Brown to stand down and not challenge him for the leadership. They struck their deal at Blair's favourite restaurant: Islington's Granita. What they didn't realise, while they chomped through their deal, was that my partner was just two tables away and couldn't wait to get home to tell me what had been going on.

You won't be surprised to discover that I don't shop at Harrods, but in that one vast store there are twelve bars and restaurants catering for all tastes and pockets, so back in 1994 a trip to dip my toes into this gastronomic delight was necessary. On the ground floor there is the delicious cheese counter, where you can sample many rare and exotic cheeses, but I decided to start at the Champagne and Oyster

Bar, with a dozen oysters followed by caviar, mozzarella and Norwegian crayfish cocktail. My friend and I then plodded upstairs to the Way In restaurant, which does light meals and drinks all day, where I could just about finish the crab cakes, but my friend could only cope with a fruit salad. Unfortunately, as we both had to go back to work, we stuck to mineral water. However, I made amends the following week when I went back with my mum to the number-one restaurant in Harrods, the Georgian. I was delighted to see that my favourite Californian wine, Robert Mondavi Fumé Blanc, was on the list, which went wonderfully with the foie gras and Sauternes jelly, whereas Mum stuck to the asparagus with walnut oil and truffles. The steak and kidney pie was magnificent, but Mum wanted the lamb fillet.

Living in north London, my favourite fish and chip shop is the Nautilus in Fortune Green. I can't remember how many times, when I was coming back late at night after the end of County Hall meetings, that I wandered home with a lovely, steaming hot bag of fish and chips. My favourite is their cod roe in matzo batter, only just a bit better than their fried scampi. They have a restaurant with really well-priced wines and I still go there with the family on the odd Friday evening

After nearly two years as a restaurant critic I was getting worried about my shape, so I sent off to two tubes of blood to the Individual Diet Company and nervously waited for their analysis of the results. They told me I was to some degree allergic or just intolerant to twenty different foods, such as courgettes, pineapple, lemon and cheese. But I was very depressed that they also listed crab, rabbit, mushrooms, chocolate, coffee, peanuts, prawns and sesame seeds, which meant the end of my passion for prawn and sesame seed toast. Most upsetting, though, was that they included brewer's yeast on the list as well as baker's yeast, so I had to give up bread, but I wasn't going to stop drinking.

Given these new dietary rules, I decided to try the Mongolian restaurant in Godalming because its menu was like it had been made to order for followers of my new diet. Allegedly, Mongolian restaurants make their food just as in the days of Genghis Khan. After a day of pillaging, raping and looting, Khan would squat down for his open-air barbecue using his upturned shield to barbecue slivers of meat and vegetables cut with his sword. I found it hard to believe that a bloodthirsty Mongolian would be contented with a mere sliver of anything.

It was a wonderful evening in which you fill your bowl with your own choice of a wide range of fish, meat and vegetables then add your favourite spices, sauces and oils. The staff then cook them in just a coupe of minutes on a vast upside-down wok over which two semi-naked Mongolians were forced to sweat. This meant you had complete control over what you were eating and I would have felt wonderful the next morning if I hadn't drunk so much as well.

Just a few weeks after I had adapted to the diet recommended by the Individual Diet Company, *Which?* magazine published a vast exposé saying it was a load of rubbish. The company challenged *Which?* and I followed the debate for a while, but can't remember who eventually won.

Some restaurants' claim to fame is based on the eccentric reputation of the chef or owner. Nico Ladenis avoided this trap, as the food he provided matched his larger-than-life reputation on London's restaurant scene. Nico was determined that his food should be the best in London. He inspected the food as it left the kitchen and also the plates as they returned to see what had been left. On one occasion an American tourist asked for ketchup and when told ketchup was banned in the restaurant, he produced a sachet from his briefcase and splattered it over his food. Nico then threw the tourist out on the street.

Chez Nico in Park Lane was relaxed and cool, so nothing interfered with your enjoyment of your meal. No music and enough space between tables for privacy. Nico greeted us at the door and immediately as we sat down, the canapés appeared on the table. Nico didn't print his menus in French, so I didn't have to go through the humiliation of asking for a translation. My guest loved the crispy salmon-finger teriyaki, and my salad of crisp guinea fowl with French beans in truffle oil and truffles was an oral orgasm. Nico's food is an artwork, with the dishes designed to combine difference of taste and texture all in one mouthful. The wine list was expensive but there was no point eating there if we were going to be worried about the bill. I thought, 'If I win the lottery, I'll eat here every week.'

I was reading an interview with the actress Lesley Joseph and was amazed when she was asked who her ideal dinner companion would be to discover it was me, particularly given she didn't like talking about politics. She said her reason for her choice was because, 'He never raises his voice. He is very gentle and contained,' so I immediately got in touch with Lesley and invited her to join me at the Ivy.

The Ivy in West Street is at the heart of London's theatre district and has been serving the theatre community since the end of the First World War. As customers need to get to the evening performances, early dinner is served from 5.30 and the restaurant is bursting with actors, agents and celebrities. The green leather benches reminded me of the House of Commons. When I visited back in 1995, the chefs Mark Hix and Des McDonald created an amazing menu based on the best Californian restaurants.

Lesley had no interest in politics and I told her that I seldom watched television and hadn't seen the programme she starred in, *Birds of a Feather*, so, faced with this cultural impasse, we decided to swap hilarious stories about previous messy relationships. Lesley introduced me to rosé champagne and by the second bottle I had a fairly good idea of how much she puts into the character of Dorien Green. The fact that I was now being paid to have lunches with actors like Lesley proved just too much for one red-faced Tory MP, who was appalled and berated me in the House of Commons.

He was most probably even more angry when he read in the next edition of *Esquire* that I had gone to lunch with the actress Cherie Lunghi. We had been doing a radio programme together and I suggested we should go out for lunch. Most people will recall her roles in *The Manageress* and *The Buccaneers*, but I was really stunned with the role she played as the lover of a left-wing Labour MP in the political drama *Bill Brand* back in 1976, when I was trying to stand for Parliament for the first time

Cherie suggested we go to the Aubergine in Chelsea, as

she liked healthy eating with steamed vegetables and very few puddings. She had a real preference for Italian food, specifically fish, which she most probably inherited from her Italian dad.

As we relaxed over coffee and petit fours, Cherie told me about her plan to develop her painting career and I told her about MPs plans to get me to retire early. Cherie was a single parent and very keen to know what Tony Blair's government would do for single parents if he won the election. But before I could reassure her about this, she had to dash off to pick up her daughter from school as I staggered back to Parliament to look for my colleagues' sympathy for my demanding workload.

In the autumn of 1995 I was overjoyed to be recruited on to the council of the Zoological Society of London. I had always loved going to London Zoo, though in those post-war years the food wasn't wonderful, but under new management there was an excellent restaurant for the society's fellows. I went to the Zoo café to meet Alexandra Dixon, who was head of the Zoo's conservation consultancy. The food was excellent, but the thing I most remember from the meal was Alexandra's story of her near death while she was tagging African elephants. The dominant female among the elephants suddenly charged at her group of conservationists, and as Alexandra fell over the elephant tried to crush her to death with its head, impaling both her arms with its tusks. In the end it threw her off several feet into the air. All my stories about the nastiness of MPs paled into insignificance.

Down by the Thames Wharf Studios is the River

Café, which had been designed as a canteen for workers at the local architects' studio. The architect was my friend Richard Rogers, who would eventually work with me when I became Mayor of London. He felt that as this bit of Hammersmith was fairly isolated, he needed to provide somewhere for his staff to get a decent meal. His wife Ruthie, in partnership with Rose Gray, decided that their Italian restaurant should set a high standard that others would struggle to achieve, and by the end of my first meal I released that they had done it by using the finest quality ingredients in imaginative new combinations.

Having both lived in northern Italy, Ruthie and Rose certainly learned how to cook great Italian meals and although they had started as amateur cooks, they produced a restaurant in which you felt you were mad not to spend at least two hours enjoying it.

Back in the seventies, Pink Floyd's Dave Gilmour and David Niven Junior opened a restaurant in Pont Street, which immediately became the place to be seen, so when Drones was reopened in November 1995 by Antony Worrall-Thompson, one of only five chefs in the UK awarded the Meilleur Ouvrier de Grande Bretagne, I was delighted at the prospect of an excellent meal in surroundings that reminded me of my dissipated youth. As you made your way through the wrought-iron gates and strode across the expensive stone floor it was pretty obvious that Worrall-Thompson had spared no expense in recreating the feel of an exclusive Iberian restaurant. He had even put lifelike lizards on the walls. Sadly, he had not sought my advice or I would have recommended the lizards he used should have been geckos, who were better at running up and down walls.

Drones, I discovered, served large portions. I had taken Mum, the only eighty-year-old I knew who thought a healthy diet was toast, tea, Cup-a-Soups and Mars bars. As she looked at the menu she said she would only be able to manage two starters, the pan-fried prawns with truffle potatoes and a warm duckling and almond Moroccan pie. Mum was shocked when the prawns turned out to be the size of small lobsters, so I had to finish them off for her.

The final restaurant I visited before *Esquire* dumped me was Mr Chow in Knightsbridge, which had opened in 1968. Back in those days I couldn't possibly have afforded a meal there, sitting alongside Orson Welles and Ingrid Bergman, who were big fans of the food. I just popped in for lunch with another MP who, like myself, desperately needed a break from the furore going on in the House of Commons at the time. The waiter recommended the chicken satay in the lightest sauce I had ever had, along with prawn sesame-seed toast, prawn rolls, crispy seaweed and smoked chicken. For the main course we had the drunken duck pancakes, which almost finished us off, but we still managed the dessert. Mr Chow's is not cheap, but it was the best Chinese meal I have had for years.

I never knew why Rosie Boycott decided to end my column, but I was really shocked decades later when Boris Johnson appointed her as his food adviser. As my days as *Esquire*'s restaurant critic came to an end, I got a surprising call from the restaurant editor of *ES* magazine (the *Evening Standard*'s Friday supplement). They asked me out of the blue to be their new weekly critic. I gladly accepted the offer with the one caveat that once a month I had to take out the restaurant editor and a colleague at *ES* and, as their offices were based in Kensington High Street, we tended to go locally.

One of the first restaurants we visited was Wodka in St Albans Grove, just off Kensington Square. Wodka (as the name suggests) was a Polish and Eastern European restaurant with the largest variety of vodka I have ever seen. We ate delicious herring blinis and pierogi dumplings, all washed down with vodka. Needless to say, I cannot remember much about the meal after the various shots of Żubrówka, Wyborów, Krupnik and many more. The one thing I *do* remember about that visit was that the Beastie Boys drove past outside very slowly in a huge limousine, at which my young political adviser, Simon, leapt up and down, fuelled by vodka and hugely excited that he had seen his favourite band.

Next up was the popular Kensington Place just off Notting Hill Gate. The majority of Associated Newspapers (owners of the *Evening Standard* and *Daily Mail*) staff lunched here on a regular basis and it would be a case of being endlessly delayed getting to our table because we had to stop and greet another editor or executive. Naturally, my politics did not fit with those of the *Standard* or the *Mail*, but we joked that I was also lunching in the 'staff canteen' of Associated Newspapers. The modern European food at Kensington Place is delicious and many times I demolished salt-and-pepper squid, steaks and scallops. The place is still thriving today, although I haven't been back to check whether it is still Associated's staff canteen.

We also ventured out of W8 to go to the Royal China in Bayswater. Here we ate endless small plates and parcels of sumptuous dim sum, delivered and devoured instantly. On this occasion there were four of us dining, including the obligatory two members of *ES* staff, and we got a bit carried away on the wine. This was a functional restaurant for the Chinese community who didn't linger over their meal, but ordered, ate and left; however, this was a Friday and we ordered bottle after bottle of wine. The staff did not raise an eyebrow at our excess, but also did not take empty bottles off the table, so to make space for the next one we put the empties on the floor. As we stood up to leave we were all shocked to see seven empty bottles under a chair. It was however, one of the best Chinese meals out I have ever had.

The surrounding roads off Kensington High Street, with beautiful Edwardian and Victorian mansions, always reminds me of spring and trees laden with blossom. The Abingdon is a charming bar and restaurant in tree-lined Abingdon Road, where I and three companions sat outside on a warm April lunchtime, appreciating the weather and eating beetroot ravioli, aged burgers and wild mushrooms on sourdough toast. This time we ordered the right amount of wine and drank ice-cold Muscadet while taking in lungfuls of blossomed air. Dining al fresco in London on an exceptionally mild spring day is one of the most pleasurable experiences in this city and now, given climate change, you can even do it in winter.

CHAPTER THIRTEEN

London Favourites

Views

I think one of the most amazing views in London is as you stand at the top of Parliament Hill on Hampstead Heath, looking south at central London. The rich history of our wonderful old buildings juxtaposed with the modernity of the new ones is awe-inspiring: a heady mix of heritage and the future combined into an incredible landscape. Dusk, as the lights twinkle on, is the best time to sit and admire it. Very close by, another good view is coming down Highgate Hill, where the City's skyscrapers spread in the distance with blinking lights and the huge Emirates Stadium, home to Arsenal Football Club, showing off its imposing and impressive arch, looms in the foreground.

On the other side of the Thames, the best view is the one from the top of the Shard; on a clear day you can see hundreds of square miles in all directions, from Watford to Sevenoaks and from Windsor Castle to Brentwood – thirty-five miles in each direction. This makes you feel like a captain of a ship discovering new lands.

The idea for the Shard was born over a lunch between the developer Irvine Sellar and the Italian architect Renzo Piano. As Irvine talked of his desire for a brand-new building above London Bridge station, Renzo sketched out his idea for the tower on a napkin. I got on well with both Renzo and Irvine because I believed that this building could transform the poor and run-down area around London Bridge. But it took until 2003 before we got the planning consent.

London Bridge is the fourth busiest railway station in the country, and at that time 50 million passengers a year went through the station. With ninety-five storeys and a height of almost a third of a kilometre, at 1,016 feet, the Shard is the tallest building in western Europe, containing offices, restaurants, a hotel, flats and five viewing platforms. As part of the development a new station concourse was constructed, and a bus station. The piles that support the building are 177 feet (fifty-four metres) deep into the soil. With forty-four lifts and 1,100 glass panels, it is truly an amazing feat of engineering. The Shard has transformed London Bridge, which is now heaving with people going to restaurants, shops, the fabulous Borough Market and clubs, whereas just a few years earlier it had been bleak and empty.

I never learned to drive, so all my life I've used public transport. I don't see any point in being caught in traffic jams when the alternative is to be able to sit on the bus or Tube and read a good book. Given I have spent almost half a century doing meetings all over London, the Tube has been a godsend. My favourite Tube line is the most recent, the Jubilee line, which took over the Bakerloo line north of Baker Street and then was extended through Green Park, Westminster, on to London Bridge and then all the way up to Stratford. Without that extension to Stratford we would never have won the Olympic bid. I was incredibly lucky to be living on the Jubilee line when Tony Blair's government decided that City Hall would be at London Bridge, so I was able to get from Willesden Green to London Bridge in about twenty-five minutes on a nice modern train.

When the Jubilee line was extended, the engineers had to dig deep under the Thames so that stations such as Canary Wharf and Canada Water are like amazing cathedrals to engineering. Stepping out of the Tube and riding the escalators up and up feels like being in a futuristic science-fiction movie. The glass screens separating the track from the platforms on this new stretch of the Jubilee line are also really handy for knowing exactly where the doors will open on the platform, something I'm very keen on!

The legacy of Herbert Morrison

I was only twenty when Herbert Morrison died in 1965, so I never met him, but because of his achievements, his funeral filled the newspapers. Before then all I knew about Morrison was that there was a nice Lambeth pub named after him, which was part of my Friday-night pub crawl around south London. There was also Herbert Morrison

House, the headquarters of the London Labour Party, just south of Elephant and Castle. Morrison was born in 1888, just a year before my grandma, in Brixton's Ferndale Road, just south of Kennington where Charlie Chaplin, a year younger, was growing up,. Morrison went to the local Stockwell school. One thing we both had in common was that the midwives at both of our births failed to clean out our eyes properly. This led to Morrison being blind in one eye all of his life. Fortunately, by the time I was born medicine had advanced massively and our doctor prescribed a few drops to clear up the mass of yellow pus in my eye.

Morrison was considered to have come from a lower-middle class family and when he left school to get a job he got completely swept up in what was then called the Independent Labour Party in Brixton in 1910. He soon became secretary of the Party, just five years later. He stood for a seat on Lambeth Council, which he lost, but then got elected as a councillor in Hackney in 1920 and went on to become Mayor of Hackney. He also got elected to the London County Council (LCC) for a seat in Woolwich in 1922. He tried to get elected as treasurer of the Labour Party at the annual conference, but was defeated by the trade-union block vote, just as I would be in 1986.

Morrison was elected an MP for South Hackney in 1923 and was the Transport Minister in Ramsay MacDonald's 1929 Labour government. It was he who introduced the legislation to create the London Passenger Transport Board, which would come into being in 1933. Sadly, Morrison lost his seat in Parliament in the Tory landslide of 1931, but that was great news for London because he then threw himself into the LCC, where he saw that Labour had its first chance of winning power. He drew up a radical manifesto and shocked the Tories by the size of his win in 1934. As leader of the LCC he unleashed a wave of policies to assist the poorest, as well as pouring money into London schools and building council housing. He changed London for ever with his Metropolitan Green Belt policy, making sure there were more protected parkland areas than anyone had ever thought possible.

His six years running County Hall were effectively a blueprint that Clement Attlee's post-war Labour government would follow. With the outbreak of war, Morrison was brought into Churchill's government as the Minister of Supply. He was often attacked in the *Daily Mail* because of his speeches, something I feel an affinity with him for. Under Attlee's government he served as deputy prime minister and as leader of the House of Commons and, eventually, foreign secretary. His grandson Peter Mandelson, said, 'He surrounded himself with experts and intellectuals who could challenge and enhance his position.' Not everyone was as nice about Morrison, including Prime Minister Attlee who described him as 'his own worst enemy'.

It's often said that the reason Attlee didn't stand down as Labour leader after Labour lost power in 1951 was because he wanted to keep Morrison from becoming Labour leader and possibly prime minster. Attlee clung on, but eventually stood down after he lost the general election in 1955, by which stage the bright young Hugh Gaitskell had emerged and decisively defeated Morrison, with 107 MPs supporting him, to just forty for Morrison. Morrison retired from the House of Commons at the end of that Parliament to become a life peer and chair of the Film Censorship Board. His role on the board was deeply conservative, with him demanding substantial cuts from the wonderful *West Side Story*. He was also appalled when the courts ruled that D. H. Lawrence's *Lady Chatterley's Lover* could be published and trenchantly opposed to the attempts to change the law making homosexuality legal. Fortunately, he was dead long before his grandson, Peter Mandelson, came out as gay. He'd asked to be called Lord Morrison of London, but he was refused by the civil servants, who claimed London was too big and important for such a title. He settled for being Baron Morrison of Lambeth. Nearly half a century later Labour MP Tony Banks would also be denied the right to claim the title of Lord Banks of London.

To read his autobiography or the much longer biography, it's quite obvious that Morrison came into politics to serve the people, not to become rich or famous. He lived in a modest home in Eltham between 1929 and 1960 and his only real indulgence was the occasional cigar. As a younger man he loved Friday-night dancing at the Co-op Women's Guild. The simple fact is almost everything that made London that amazing post-war city comes from the legacy of the work he started on the LCC in the 1930s. Like the lives of every other Londoner, my life was transformed for the better because of him.

Monuments

My favourite monument is the statue of Nelson Mandela in Parliament Square. Back in the days when I was leader of the GLC, Mandela was still in prison in South Africa when we commissioned a small bust of Mandela from the sculptor Ian Walters. Walters had to imagine what Mandela looked like, because no new photograph had been published since he was imprisoned in 1964, twenty years earlier. The bust was unveiled on the side of the Southbank Centre, though at the time Thatcher denounced it because she claimed we were supporting terrorists, and Tories on Westminster Council were wearing T-shirts saying 'Hang Nelson Mandela'.

It was just a few years later, in February 1990, that I sat gripped, waiting to see the broadcast of Mandela marching over the hilltop following his release from prison. Four years later he would become the first black president of South Africa. Back then, I would never have guessed that in 2005, as we bid for the Olympics, we would be broadcasting an endorsement of our bid by Mandela. By the time I was mayor there was a growing demand for a full sculpture of Mandela to be placed in Trafalgar Square. The idea came from campaigning journalist Donald Woods and the money for the statue was raised by Sir Richard Attenborough. Once again, we commissioned Ian Walters to create it, but Westminster Council bitterly opposed having the statue in Trafalgar Square. Eventually, after a meeting with Deputy Prime Minister John Prescott, and the Tory leader of Westminster Council, Simon Milton, we were finally able to get agreement from Westminster Council for the statue to go up in Parliament Square. Without the pressure from John Prescott, Westminster would never have given planning permission for it to be built.

One of my key aides, Redmond O'Neill, who was having to cope with an exhausting regime of chemotherapy for his cancer, worked tirelessly to organise the unveiling of the statue on 29 August 2007. Parliament Square was packed with 7,000 people, including anti-apartheid campaigners, diplomats, Richard Attenborough, Jesse Jackson, Tony Benn, Ben Okri, Naomi Campbell and even David Cameron. Given Boris Johnson had warned that 'South Africa under Mandela's leadership is a tyranny of black rule', he didn't bother to come.

As the frail Mandela slowly came into the square, most of the audience were in tears. Prime Minister Gordon Brown and I unveiled the statue and I pointed out that Mandela was sharing this square with Abraham Lincoln, who freed the slaves, and Churchill, who led a nation standing alone against the evil of Nazi ideology. Mandela told us he first came to Parliament Square with Oliver Tambo in 1962 and the young lawyers joked that they hoped to one day see a statue of a black person in the square alongside the existing one of the South African leader General Jan Smuts, who became the prime minster in 1939, in a country where the black majority were treated as second-class citizens even before it got worse with the imposition of apartheid.

Fantasy dinner-party guests

I would love nothing more than to be able to have a dinner party at Vasco & Piero's Pavilion in Poland Street with the people I have most admired since I got interested in politics. One would be President John Kennedy. It was his assassination in 1963 that changed my life. All that weekend I was glued to the television and started to learn about American politics for the first time. It led me to start reading about US politics and, eventually, English politics, which in turn led me to join the Labour Party, rather than carrying on breeding tropical frogs and toads.

Although Kennedy started out with quite a right-wing agenda, with one of his 1960 election promises being to close the missile gap with the Soviet Union, he rapidly changed and began to throw the weight of his administration behind the struggle to end racism in America's Deep South. Also, he was planning to withdraw American troops from Vietnam if re-elected in 1964, because he realised a full-scale war in Vietnam would be a disaster.

What changed his politics so much were his conflicts with the military. He had only been president a few days before they got him to continue with the planned invasion of Cuba by a small band of Cuban dissidents. The military told him that the invasion would lead to an uprising and the overthrow of Fidel Castro, so America would not need to provide any air support for the invasion of the Bay of Pigs. But no sooner had the rebels landed than the Pentagon was insisting that Kennedy agree to American air strikes on Cuba. Kennedy realised he has been lied to and refused.

I would love to be able to go back in time and tell him that Castro's regime would outlast the reign of twelve US presidents, eight of whom, including Kennedy, authorised assassination attempts on Castro, all of which failed.

Kennedy had already been shocked to discover that his campaign pledge to close the missile gap with Russia was nonsense. At his first military briefing he was told that the Soviet Union had four nuclear missiles capable of landing in the USA, whereas the USA had 350 capable of obliterating the Soviet Union. It says a lot about the way we are lied to by governments that a man who had been a senator for eight years and was on the verge of becoming president was as completely ignorant about the truth of America's nuclear superiority as were all the rest of us. Kennedy's predecessor, Republican President Eisenhower, had tried to warn the American people about the growth of the power of the military in his final television address before his presidency ended, but nothing has changed and, if anything, the military has gained more power over the American government today than it had back then, when 50 per cent of the federal budget was spent on the military.

At my dinner party with Kennedy, as well as asking him what it was he learned that made him decide to withdraw from Vietnam, I would want to know about his plans to try and end the Cold War with Russia, which he spelled out in his June 1963 speech. If he hadn't been assassinated it wouldn't just have saved the lives of over 3 million Vietnamese, but we could have seen an end to the Cold War, with all those billions and billions spent on the military–industrial complex being used to make a better world both in America and elsewhere. I would also want to ask him if he really believed that it was only Lee Harvey Oswald responsible for his death or could it have been the military–industrial complex, who dreaded that an end to the Cold War would lose them billions of dollars a year. I also would want to know what attracted him to Marilyn Monroe.

Another person I would want to have at my dinner is Franklin Delano Roosevelt, widely seen as the greatest US president in history. Just as the world was affected by Kennedy's premature death, it would be very different if FDR hadn't died just three weeks before the surrender of Germany in 1945. Roosevelt had been a transforming president, coming to power in the depths of the Great Depression of the 1930s with his pledge for a New Deal. Perhaps the most important legislation he passed was the Glass–Steagall act, which made it illegal for the local high-street banks to get involved in risky speculation like the so-called investment banks. This created over sixty years of stable banking until the act was repealed by President Clinton at the end of his administration, which opened the path to the banking crash of 2008. FDR lifted America's economy with a massive increase in public-sector investment in projects like the Tennessee Valley Authority. Of course, he attracted virulent criticism from the far right and the rich. When he introduced benefits for the unemployed, Republicans and the right-wing press were screaming that this was 'the first step to communism'. Had he not died, he would have delivered on his promise for America to create a national health service, but his biggest legacy would have been to avoid forty-five years of Cold War.

There were two wartime conferences at which Stalin, Churchill and Roosevelt met, and I think it quite significant that at both of them Roosevelt organised one-to-one meetings with Stalin to which Churchill wasn't invited. By the end of the Yalta conference in February 1945, Roosevelt realised there could be a good working relationship with Stalin. FDR always expressed a high opinion of Stalin and Stalin did not hide his fondness for FDR. Details of this potentially transforming relationship can be found in Simon Sebag Montefiore's biography of Stalin. Stalin had wanted to borrow $6 billion from America to help rebuild his ravaged country. FDR also agreed with Stalin that the era of colonialism had to come to an end, particularly for Britain's biggest colony, India, which is most probably why Churchill wasn't invited to the meetings. He and Stalin agreed that after the defeat of Japan, French Indo-China should be granted independence, which would have avoided the horrific wars of Vietnam, Cambodia and Laos over the next thirty years.

I would be interested to know how much of his radical politics came from contracting of polio when he was thirty-nine. This devastating illness must have changed the way this fabulously wealthy man saw the world and helped him understand the needs of the poorest. I would also want to know how he planned to work with Stalin. Just a couple of days before his death, he had sent a telegram to Churchill saying they shouldn't be distracted by their differences of opinion with Stalin; these disagreements could usually be resolved and Roosevelt had no doubt they could work together after the war. And I'd be interested to know what he thought about the damage done by the Cold War. Did he also regret having the affair that almost destroyed his marriage to the formidable Eleanor Roosevelt?

The third guest round the table would be Bobby Kennedy, who, if he hadn't been assassinated in 1968, would have brought the war in Vietnam to an end. He started out even further to the right than his elder brother but, like Jack Kennedy, he moved to a much more progressive set of policies once he became his brother's attorney general. He played a crucial role in challenging the racism endemic in the Deep South. Following the president's assassination, the new president, Johnson, excluded Bobby Kennedy from any influence in his government. Bobby then ran for senator in New York and spent the rest of his life campaigning for justice for the poorest and most neglected. Just as with his brother, I would be interested to ask Bobby if there was any truth to the rumour that he was with Marilyn Monroe earlier on the day that she took her own life.

If these three men had not died when they did, the world today would be a much better place. That might also be true of my next guest, Vladimir Lenin. Lenin's presence might come as quite a shock to the three Americans, but he would have a lot to say about what happened in Russia after his death.

When Lenin seized power in the 1917 Russian Revolution, he believed revolutions were about to break out all the way across Europe and the world as a consequence of the war, but as a few years passed and that didn't happen, he recognised he had to follow a different agenda. He introduced a New Economic Plan, which allowed a private sector to exist alongside the nationalised economy. An attempted assassination in 1918 left him with a bullet embedded in his body, which it is thought may have been a factor in his early death. He'd only been running Russia for a few years before his first stroke on May 1922 meant he had to leave running the country to his colleagues. He became alarmed at the behaviour of Joseph Stalin, and just before his death from a third stroke in January 1924 he had sent a letter to the Central Committee urging them to remove Stalin from power. Had Lenin not died, millions more Russians would have had their lives saved from Stalin's horrific policies, which led to mass murder, mainly of peasants, but also many fellow communists.

Finally, to lighten it up a bit, I would also like to have David Attenborough present. David became my hero when I began watching his animal programmes on the BBC in the late 1950s and as well as day dreaming of becoming an astronaut, I also wanted to become another David Attenborough. I had a meal with him while I was mayor and it was one of the best and most interesting conversations I had ever had. Not only is David a really nice guy, but he has a complete grasp of what climate change is doing to our world. The other guests would all be amazed to discover that we are now living in a world where the greatest threat to our existence isn't nuclear weapons but rising temperatures.

CHAPTER FOURTEEN

Londoners

The most important books I read in terms of their impact on me as a twelve-year-old were science fiction such as the remarkable *Brave New World* by Aldous Huxley, but even more significant were George Orwell's *Nineteen Eighty-Four* and *Animal Farm*. Although he had been born in India, Orwell was brought up in England and spent much of his time in London (after attending Eton), mainly living at several addresses in Hampstead, where he worked as an assistant in a bookshop just before he left to fight for the republicans in the Spanish Civil War at the end of 1936. He was later a BBC radio producer and worked as war correspondent for the *Observer* as well as on the socialist magazine *Tribune*.

Although he died just a year after I was born, my favourite author during my teens was H. G. Wells, who had been born in conservative Bromley and went on to study at the Royal College of Science, now part of Imperial College

London, where he was deeply influenced by the lecturer T. H. Huxley. I remember falling in love with his books after my parents took me to see the films based on *The Time Machine* and *The War of the Worlds*. He also wrote about history and I adored the old copy of *The Outline of History* that my uncle had given me. Wells lived on the borders of Regent's Park and was furious when the Royal Society refused to offer him a fellowship. This may have been because of his support for free love and the fact that he shared the Russian baroness Moura Budberg as a mistress with writer Maxim Gorky. There were also rumours of his affair with novelist Rebecca West. Although he wrote his own obituary in 1936, he went on to live for another decade.

Both Wells and Orwell have blue plaques on the homes where they used to live (Wells is at 13 Hanover Terrace, NW1 and Orwell's is at 50 Lawford Road, NW5) and across London there are over 800 of these plaques commemorating some of the most important people ever to live and work in London. Many were Londoners, but many were changed and even transformed when they came to London. The first plaque was put up in 1866 by the Royal Society of Arts; the project was then taken over by the LCC and carried on by the GLC until it was abolished, and since then this has been the work of English Heritage.

Although D. H. Lawrence died in 1930, we had to wait until 1969 before a plaque was put up in his honour at 1 Byron Villas, NW3. This is most probably because he was such a provocative writer. He had always had a controversial career, particularly when one of his most brilliant works,

The Rainbow, was taken out of publication because of the accusations of obscenity. This triggered a depression and he moved from London to Cornwall, where he was accused of being a German spy because he was married to a German woman. Forced to move yet again, and with the controversy over *Lady Chatterley's Lover*, which was suppressed and not published until 1961, he left Britain for Europe.

At 48 Doughty Street, WC1 you can see the plaque of Charles Dickens, put up in 1903 by the LCC. He grew up in Camden and his father was sent to debtors' prison when he was just twelve, so he started work in a blacking (boot polish) factory, which meant a four-mile walk to and from work each day. Before he moved to Doughty Street in 1837, Dickens was living in Holborn, paying the amazing rent of £80 per year, but he was making quite a bit of money from the instalments he'd published of *The Pickwick Papers* and *Oliver Twist*. As his money built up, he was able to buy a bigger home for his family at 1 Devonshire Terrace in Marylebone.

An even sadder story than that about D. H. Lawrence is about another writer, Sylvia Plath. Like Plath, many of the people honoured with the blue plaques didn't come from London. She had grown up in the USA and came in the mid-1950s as a Fulbright Scholar to Cambridge, where at a drunken party she met and soon, in secret, married fellow poet Ted Hughes in December 1959. Her plaque is at 3 Chalcot Square, NW1. Although outwardly she had a happy life and was producing her amazing novel *The Bell Jar*, she had a long-running problem with depression. Following her separation from Hughes, she moved to 23 Fitzroy Road with her two very young children, but took her own life there three months later. She chose this address, which obviously has no blue plaque for Plath, because it already had the blue plaque of W. B. Yeats.

Another author who led a troubled life was Oscar Wilde, whose plaque can be found at 34 Tite Street in Chelsea. His lifestyle and wit defined his public reputation and his first novel, *The Picture of Dorian Grey*, was followed by the plays *Lady Windermere's Fan*, *The Importance of Being Earnest* and many others. While he was married with two children he was also in love with the poet John Gray. However, tragically, it was Wilde's love for the son of the Marquess of Queensberry that tipped him into a huge public controversy when he sued the Marquess for calling him 'a ponce and sodomite'. Having lost the case, he was then prosecuted and imprisoned for homosexuality for two years at Reading Gaol. When he was released from prison he went, just like Lawrence, to live the rest of his life in Europe. When Parliament voted to make homosexuality illegal during the reign of Queen Victoria, the law was only passed with a majority of one vote. Had just one other MP changed their mind, Wilde would have had a very different and better life.

Perhaps one of the most controversial writers to be awarded a plaque was C. L. R. James. Born in Trinidad, he lived in London several times, the last being from 1981 until his death in 1989. He first came to England much earlier, in 1932, and reported on cricket for the *Manchester Guardian*. Just before the Second World War he wrote *The Black Jacobins* then he went off to the USA and joined a Trotskyist party. He was deported from the USA and then also placed under house arrest while he was in Trinidad by the Prime Minister of Trinidad Eric Williams who had been one of his pupils when he was teaching. When he returned to London in 1953, he was living just around the corner from where I now live in Willesden. James was loved by the West Indian communities in Britain but became virtually housebound in a little second-floor flat in Brixton before his death. His plaque was finally unveiled during Black History Month in 2004 by his nephew Darcus Howe at 165 Railton Road, SW24.

At 22b Ebury Street, SW1 is the plaque that commemorates Ian Fleming, who died relatively young but was world famous for creating James Bond. Born in London and educated at Eton, Fleming went on to serve as senior naval intelligence officer in the 1950s. In 1953 I became a fan when the *Daily Express* ran a series of his Bond novels as comic strips, but as soon as his books started appearing in paperback I could afford to buy them and I bought them all. My dad loved reading them as well. What we did not know was that Fleming's wife Ann was for years having an affair with the leader of the Labour Party, Hugh Gaitskell. Back in those days the establishment looked after its own and the press didn't go poking around in the private lives of the elite. Gaitskell's affair was never mentioned in the press even though there was a photograph of him drunk, hanging on to a lamp post and being propped up by Ann Fleming. Another great character of the time, Bob Boothby, was for years having an affair with Prime Minister Harold MacMillan's wife. The elite all knew but the public were kept in the dark. It was only after the Profumo affair erupted that the press started to change its approach. Up until then the only time an MP's sexual adventures had been exposed was on a couple of occasions when gay MPs were arrested by the police for having sex in public toilets or parks.

The final author I would chose wasn't a Londoner but chose London as a place of refuge and that is commemorated with a plaque at 122 Church Road, SE19 by Crystal Palace, where Emile Zola stayed. Perhaps the greatest French author, he produced a series of twenty novels about the life of a family in the second French empire. At the age of fifty-seven Zola was caught up in the Dreyfus affair – a French Jewish officer accused of treason – and Zola leapt to his defence. Zola was then found guilty of libel but escaped and fled to London in 1898. While staying at a hotel in Walton, he was tracked down by the *Daily Mail* and so disappeared to the Queen's Hotel in Church Road, Norwood where he took on a new persona and called himself Mr Richard. One of Zola's main pleasures was just cycling in and around Crystal Palace. When Dreyfus won the right to be retried, Zola rushed back to France in 1899, where he was pardoned, and died just two years later.

While many of the 800 honoured with a plaque were born and raised in London, many, like Zola, came here to seek refuge or a good education. Many others had been born somewhere in the rest of Britain. One of those who migrated to London and fell in love with it was one of the greatest scientists of all time, Sigmund Freud. His plaque is at 20 Maresfield Gardens, NW3. Freud had fled from Vienna after its seizure by Hitler and arrived in London in June 1938. As the founder of psychoanalysis, he changed the lives not just of his own patients, but millions of others around the world as his breathtaking work in psychiatry was taken up all over the planet. His home is now the Freud Museum, which is an amazing homage to Freud and his daughter Anna, with a very nice garden attached.

A giant of even greater standing is of course Charles Darwin, whose plaque can be found at 110 Gower Street, WC1, where he lived between 1838 and 1842, shortly before he wrote *On the Origin of Species*, which spelled out the way evolution had determined all life on the planet. Although he believed his theory of evolution was true, he recognised that in a predominantly deeply religious world challenging the Bible in this way would unleash a storm of criticism, so he didn't publish it until over a decade later, in1858. Darwin had fallen in love with London, writing about the 'grandeur about its smoky fogs, and the dull, distant sounds of cabs and coaches; in fact you may perceive I am becoming a thoroughly paced Cockney'.

Of all the plaques across London perhaps the man who had the greatest influence on all our lives is John Maynard Keynes, the economist who created the economic strategy based on investment and public spending that led to thirty years of strong economic growth across the Western post-war world, giving my generation the best quality of life in human history. His book *The General Theory of Employment, Interest and Money* was published in 1936 and makes him the most significant economist since the first giant of economics, Adam Smith. His plaque can be found at 46 Gordon Square, WC1 where he lived from 1916. The home was actually owned by Clive and Vanessa Bell, good friends of Virginia Woolf. They were all part of the radical Bloomsbury Group, but for some reason no official blue plaque has ever been put up to commemorate where this group held their meetings, so it was left to Camden Council to honour them at 51 Gordon Square.

As I said earlier, my favourite view in London is from Parliament Hill, and it was the painter John Constable who produced several watercolours in his home at 40 Well Walk in Hampstead where he wrote: 'Our little drawing room commands a view unsurpassed in Europe, from Westminster Abbey to Gravesend.' Many of his sketches show the effects of the weather and light from the Hampstead landscape,

Another person whose life was partly defined by moving to London was Friedrich Engels. Although born in Germany, he came here at the age of twenty-two, first working in Manchester, where he became a socialist and started to write books like *The Condition of the Working Class in England* which came out in 1845, the year after he had first met Karl Marx, who then collaborated with him to write *The Communist Manifesto*. His plaque can be found by Regent's Park at 122 Regent's Park Road, where he had moved so he could be close to Marx, who was living at Haverstock Hill in Hampstead.

There are of course plaques commemorating our prime ministers and politicians, but most people today will never have heard of Sir Stafford Cripps, who died in 1952 just after the fall of the post-war Labour government. His plaque stands at 32 Elm Park Gardens, SW10 where he was born in 1889. His father, Baron Cripps, held office in the first two Labour governments under Ramsay MacDonald. Cripps himself only got involved in politics in his late thirties; before that he had been the youngest King's Counsel in Britain. Churchill sent him to be our ambassador to Russia during the Second World War and after Labour won the 1945 election, he was president of the Board of Trade. Two years later, the Chancellor of the Exchequer, Hugh Dalton, was forced to resign because an *Evening Standard* journalist asked him about the contents of the budget he would announce later that day. The paper broke the news just before he got up to announce the budget and he was forced to submit his resignation for having leaked it. When you think what MPs get away with today without being forced to resign, this looks like a more severe era. Stafford Cripps took over the most important job in the cabinet and laid the foundation for the rebuilding of our post-war economy, including finding the money for the NHS, house building, more teachers, and pensions and welfare benefits.

At 98 Cheyne Walk in Chelsea is the plaque of Isambard Kingdom Brunel, one of our greatest civil engineers. His father had built the first tunnel under the Thames between Wapping and Rotherhithe, which is now used by the East London train line. His fame and his legacy are for the building of the Great Western Railway and designing the Clifton Suspension Bridge in Bristol as well as constructing giant steamships, such as the *Great Eastern*.

While many of these plaques recognise people born abroad who then achieve greatness in London, with some it is the other way around. Alfred Hitchcock, whose plaque is at 153 Cromwell Road, SW5 was born in Leytonstone. At the age of twenty-six he produced his first film, *The*

Pleasure Garden in 1925, followed by *Blackmail*, which was the first full-length talkie film. Even better remembered are *The Thirty-Nine Steps* in 1935 and *The Lady Vanishes* in 1938. By March 1939 he had become disillusioned with the poor artistic levels of cinema in this country and defected to Hollywood, where he became a US citizen in 1955 and produced a raft of films that were successes around the world and were inspiring for my post-war generation.

Many of the people who brought about the end of the colonialism of the great European powers came to London either to escape imprisonment or just to get a good education. The first to achieve independence for a country in Africa was Kwame Nkrumah, whose plaque can be found at 60 Burghley Road in Kentish Town. Nkrumah was born in 1909 in what was then our colony the Gold Coast, now known as Ghana. He arrived in London just before the end of the Second World War in 1945 to study philosophy, but got swept up in political campaigning. Before the end of the year he had become vice-president of the West African Students' Union, joint secretary of the Fifth Pan-African Congress and regional secretary of the Pan-African Federation. His earliest memory of London was the problems he had trying rent a room, because of his colour, until he was finally accepted at Burghley Road, where his landlady took him in as part of the family. In November 1947 he returned to the Gold Coast and began the campaign for independence. He succeeded in 1957, thus unleashing a tide of change that would bring an end to all the old empires over the next quarter century.

Another significant campaigner against the racism that was so endemic back in those days was Paul Robeson, one of the earliest black singers and actors to become world famous. He lived at 1 Branch Hill in Hampstead between 1929 and 1930 after his triumph with the musical *Showboat*, which was first performed in London. He is still remembered for his amazing performance of 'Old Man River'. Perhaps his greatest achievement was in *Othello* at the Savoy Theatre, a production that crossed the Atlantic to appear on Broadway in 1943. There it was to become the longest-running Shakespearean performance in history. He campaigned actively against fascism, racism and colonialism, which made him a target of the American far-right senator Joseph McCarthy in the early 1950s. This led him to leave the USA for London. The original hope was to put his plaque up at 19 Buckingham Street, WC2 where he lived in the 1930s, but the owners refused.

A figure of great controversy was Sylvia Pankhurst, whose plaque is at 120 Cheyne Walk in Chelsea. She was arrested and imprisoned far too many times to list them all here, but had become the predominant figure in the campaign for a woman's right to vote. Her decision to have a child with the man she was living with but refusing to marry tore her family apart and created widespread condemnation publicly. She lived long enough to see women getting the right to vote, but not long enough to see the first female prime minister because she died in 1960.

A blue plaque at 13 Lyme Street NW1 commemorates two of the great allies of Nelson Mandela, Joe Slovo and Ruth First. Nineteen and twenty years older than me, they had spent all their adult life fighting against apartheid in South Africa. They met Mandela at university shortly before they married in 1949 and what put their lives at risk was not just that they were fighting against apartheid, but they were both white and seen as traitors for campaigning under the slogan 'South African belongs to all who live in it, black and white'. They fought a charge of treason in 1956 and won. But Ruth was imprisoned in 1963 and came here when she was released. Joe was charged with treason in 1961 but escaped. For twelve years they lived at Lyme Street, writing and campaigning, until Ruth was killed by a letter bomb sent by the South African racist government. Joe survived long enough to fight on to the defeat of apartheid and was a key player in negotiating that. He was the minister for housing in Nelson Mandela's government and the plaque was unveiled in 2003 by Mandela.

Few people have had a greater impact in the fight for justice for black slaves than William Wilberforce, perhaps the most significant opponent of slavery. He became the MP for Hull in 1780 and campaigned for nineteen years to achieve the abolition of slavery in the West Indies in 1807. He lived in London at 44 Cadogan Place, SW1, where he died in 1833. He campaigned against slavery while he was living in Battersea Rise, and he succeeded when the bill abolishing slavery throughout the British Empire was passed in 1833, just before his death.

Not all of those who came to London while fighting for freedom in the British Empire left a good legacy. Muhammad Ali Jinnah was born in Pakistan in 1876 and at the age of sixteen was here in London, living at 35 Russell

Road, W14, studying law before he qualified for the Bar four years later, when he was just nineteen. He returned to what was then British India and began campaigning for an independent Muslim state in what is now Bangladesh and Pakistan. He bitterly resisted the efforts of the Labour MP Sir Stafford Cripps, who was sent to India in 1942 to try and achieve a united independent India that included Muslims and Hindus. When Britain gave in to the demand for separation and granted independence to India and Pakistan in 1947, Jinnah became the governor general just a year before he died. Tragically, splitting Britain's old Indian empire into rival Muslim and Hindu states would lead to endless conflict and three wars.

The first prime minister of India, Jawaharlal Nehru, came from a rich family who could afford to send him to Harrow public school and Cambridge University before he also, like Jinnah, studied to become a barrister at the Inner Temple. He spent many evenings gambling and visiting London's theatres and swilling down champagne over supper at the Savoy Hotel. In those years it is unlikely that people would have believed Nehru would one day become the decisive socialist politician that forced Britain to give up its largest colony. By 1929 he had changed and announced that he was both a socialist and wanted an Indian republic and spent the rest of his life working with Mahatma Gandhi and all the others fighting for independence. He was sent to prison several times by Britain, first in 1921, and spent eighteen of the next twenty-five years in jail, but he became India's first prime minster and ruled the nation from 1947 to 1964, always advocating peace between the West and the

Soviet Union. His plaque can be found at 60 Elgin Crescent in Notting Hill.

Gandhi's plaque is not far away, at 20 Barons Court Road, W14. Like Nehru, Gandhi was also in London studying law, becoming a member of the Inner Temple at the age of just nineteen. He took dancing lessons and insisted on only going to vegetarian restaurants. His love of London was obvious when he said that apart form India, 'I would rather live in London than any other place in the world.' Like Nehru, he was imprisoned by the British many times. He did not just want independence for India, but an India that would abolish the appalling caste system. In 1948 he was assassinated by a Hindu extremist. Gandhi also has a plaque at Kingsley Hall in Bow, E3, where he worked for the poor.

Another person whose legacy has been the division of one of our colonies along religious lines is Chaim Weizmann. Although he started life as a scientist, he went on to become the first president of Israel. He had been born in Russia in 1874 but came here in 1904, and became a British citizen while teaching at Manchester University. A decade later he moved to London and his plaque is at 67 Anderson Road, W14 where he was a key player in helping Britain win the First World War by discovering how to increase the production of explosives. Weizmann became the leading activist in the Zionist movement and was crucial in persuading the British government in 1917 to announce that Jews would be allowed to return to Palestine. He was a key player in the struggle to divide Palestine into Jewish and Arab sectors when Britain withdrew in 1948. The GLC wanted his plaque to be at 16 Addison Crescent, W14, where he lived for nineteen years between the two world wars, but this was 1974 and the owner feared that the Yom Kippur War, just a few months earlier, which led to the Middle East oil crisis, would draw attention and perhaps lead to an attack on the property.

In Canterbury Crescent in Brixton a plaque commemorates Havelock Ellis. Born in Croydon, he moved to Australia before returning to London to become a doctor at St Thomas's Hospital. He researched and went on to publish the seven volumes of *Studies in the Psychology of Sex* between 1897 and 1928, which were banned in the UK. His whole life was surrounded by controversy because he advocated sexual freedom, including for gay people, during the Victorian era. His wife was bisexual, which was also not considered acceptable under Victoria's reign, and he became the leading pioneer in researching the psychology of sex and defending same-sex attraction.

Two people who would have a profound influence in creating the world in which we now live were Sidney and Beatrice Webb, whose plaque is at 10 Netherhall Gardens in Hampstead. Both were historians, but their real legacy came from their political activities. Sidney was an early member of the Fabian Society and served as a London county councillor, and he helped to found the London School of Economics, and with Beatrice and others set up the *New Statesman* magazine. Sidney also served in the first two Labour governments but both went on to spend considerable time visiting and writing about the Soviet Union. Sidney died in 1947, just four years after Beatrice, but their work in helping to build the Labour Party helped lay the foundation for the achievements of the post-war Labour government.

An even more profound legacy is that of Sir Alexander Fleming, who lived for thirty-five years until his death in 1955 at 20a Danvers Street, SW3 where his plaque now stands. He had been born in Scotland and became a doctor in 1906, and hundreds of millions of people would not be alive today were it not for his work as a bacteriologist at St Mary's Hospital in Paddington where, in 1928, he discovered penicillin.

Another man whose work has transformed our world is Alan Turing. His birthplace in 1912 is now marked by his English Heritage plaque at 2 Warrington Crescent, W9. After studying science at Cambridge, at the age of twenty-four Turing published a crucial paper 'On Computable Numbers' in 1936, which created what became known as the 'universal Turing machine': the origin of the modern computer. He played a vital role in the Second World War by deciphering the German Enigma code at Bletchley Park in Bedfordshire, for which he was rewarded at OBE. With the war over, Turing was a central player in creating the world's first universal computer, but tragically in those intolerant times he became a victim of homophobia when he was prosecuted for having sex with another man. He was sentenced to undergo 'chemical castration', which made him impotent and saw his breasts grow to be like those of a woman. Depressed and unable to return to his work, he killed himself by pouring cyanide on an apple in 1954. The half-eaten apple was found by his dead body, which is why that computer company adopted the name and logo.

Back in 1964 the LCC unveiled a plaque at the junction of Edgware Road and Bayswater Road, W2, but not to commemorate a person. This is the site of the Tyburn Tree, where thousands of public executions took place from 1196 until the last public hanging (of the highwayman John Austin) on 3 November 1783. Along with the thousands of people who were hanged there, Oliver Cromwell's dead body was dug up so he could hang from the branches of the Tyburn Tree after the restoration of the monarchy. So many people were hanged back in the sixteenth century that the trees couldn't cope on their own, so a massive gallows was constructed in order for up to twenty-four people could be hanged at once.

The way in which London transformed people who came here from abroad is, I think, revealed by the comments above by Darwin and Gandhi when they talk about their love of our city. If you are interested in all the other plaques around London, there is a brilliant book by Emily Cole, published by English Heritage, called *Lived in London*, which lists all our great city's 800 plaques.

CHAPTER FIFTEEN

Who Runs the World?

Earlier in the book I talked about how the City of London Corporation had maintained its independence from the rest of London for over 1,000 years, with the result that to a degree it is outside the control of the laws and institutions of the rest of the UK. The City recently stated that 'it is the oldest continuous municipal democracy in the world ... routed in the ancient rights and privileges enjoyed by citizens before the Norman Conquest of 1066'. Maurice Glasman, a lecturer in political theory at Guildhall University, said, 'The City's powers have waxed and waned over the centuries but overall it has remained a political fortress withstanding the tides of history that has transformed the rest of the British nation state. Its special privileges stem ultimately from the power of financial capital. Britain's rulers have needed the City's money and given the City what it wants in exchange.'

Modern Britain has no written constitution, but Glasman

lists four basic pillars that pass for our ancient constitu-tion: the monarch as its head, the Church as its soul, the Parliament as the country and the City as the money, but only subordinate to the Crown and Parliament up to a limited point.

When William the Conqueror seized Britain in 1066 the City kept its ancient liberties and self-organising militias, so whenever the king entered the City he had to disarm. Following the Protestant Reformation, the power of the monarch declined and Parliament slowly mutated from being a collection of aristocrats as the right to vote was slowly wid-ened to, eventually, all adults. These were major changes but did not affect the City, which retained its privileges.

Over the centuries there have been several unsuccessful attempts to reform the City. Following the creation of the Labour Party, one of its central planks was its opposition to the City and in particular the independent Bank of England. The future LCC leader Herbert Morrison said towards the end of the First World War, 'Is it not time London faced up to the pretentious buffoonery of the City and wipe it of the municipal map? The City is now a square mile of entrenched reaction, the home of the devilry of modern finance and that journalistic abortion, the stunt press. The City is an administrative anachronism.'

Over the decades that followed the Labour Party con-tinued to pledge to abolish the Corporation and include it in the wider London government. Labour's current shadow chancellor, John McDonnell, said, 'The traditional Labour position was to control the finances of the country in the long-term interests of its people.'

In the run-up to the 1945 election Labour leader Clement Attlee said, 'Over and over again we have seen that there is in this country another power than that which has its seat at Westminster. The City of London, a convenient term for a collection of financial interests, is able to assert itself against the government of the country. Those who control money can pursue a policy at home and abroad contrary to that which has been decided by the people. The first step in the transfer of this power is the conversion of the Bank of England into a state institution.'

When the Bank of England was created in 1694 it was largely to provide credit for building our navy, and ushered in a financial revolution that led to the creation of mortgage markets, Lloyds of London insurance, a stock exchange, a financial press and the rapid expansion of overseas trade. But although Attlee's government did nationalise the bank in 1946, the bank had powerful cards to play, in particular its control over the nation's money. Interestingly, when Labour lost the 1951 election, Winston Churchill's government did not repeal the nationalisation of the bank. That may well be because Churchill had discovered that during the Second World War the governor of the Bank of England had transferred a substantial proportion of Britain's gold reserves to Nazi Germany because we owed them the gold, but the governor of the bank never consulted the government before he did this.

Despite its nationalisation, the bank it continued to be run by the same group of old Etonian merchant bankers, and although the government had acquired powers to issue directions to the bank, it admitted in 2010 that, 'Thus far the power has not been used.' Even more disappointing was the failure of the Attlee government to absorb the City into the London County Council. Over a decade later, when the Tory government set up a royal commission to consider the creation of the Greater London Council, the commission's report stated, 'Logic has its limits and the position of the City lies outside them.'

When Harold Wilson's Labour government was elected in 1964 and discovered that our trade deficit was twice what the outgoing Tories had admitted, he gave in to pressure from the bank's governor to slash most of his spending promises, causing him to say, 'Who is prime minister of this country Mr Governor, you or me?'

Some Chancellors of the Exchequer have been a bit firmer with the bank than Wilson was. When Tory Ken Clarke became chancellor after Britain's eviction from the Exchange Rate Mechanism in 1992, he constantly resisted the almost monthly demand from the governor to increase interest rates. Ken represented a constituency with a still substantial manufacturing sector and he knew increasing interest rates may very well benefit the financial sector but usually damaged our manufacturing.

Increasing interest rates has an impact on driving up unemployment and while the post-war Attlee government kept interest rates to 2 per cent and unemployment fell to its lowest level in the post-war era, most Tory and Labour governments have given in to the demand for an increase in interest rates, which means we have never been able to get our unemployment down to the level of 1951.

While the City continues to be a vastly powerful

institution, it was transformed by Thatcher when she pushed through a massive deregulation of the financial sector in 1986. Before then the City was dominated by the old Etonian elite; now it became overwhelmed by foreign financiers descending and turning it into a genuinely more international institution.

When Tony Blair became Labour's leader he did a deal with the City promising them not to increase regulation of their powers and practices. This therefore made it easier for him to win the next election without opposition from the financial sector funding the Tories. Blair had effectively turned the Labour Party into a vehicle the City fell in love with and finally scrapped Labour's long-term commitment to incorporate the City into a Greater London Authority.

Even more bizarre was Blair's decision to change the balance of votes inside the City. Before Blair came to power 8,000 residents living in the City had one vote each but businesses in the City could vote as well, and had 23,000 votes between them. Blair allowed them to increase their votes to 32,000. The *Guardian* pointed out that he was giving companies 'carte blanche to run the City'. Now the Bank of China, Moscow's Narodny Bank, KPMG and Goldman Sachs are voting in British elections. Tony Benn was one of a few Labour MPs who opposed this, saying, 'We are considering a corrupt proposal, we are being asked to legalise the buying of votes for political purposes. The City is an offshore island moored in the Thames with a freedom that many other offshore islands would be glad to have.'

After the Second World War the creation of the Eurodollar market allowed US banks to shift money to

London in order to avoid the restrictions placed on them in the USA. Britain made matters worse when it allowed many of its former small colonies to become tax havens. Just one building in the Cayman Islands is the legal headquarters for 12,000 corporations. In just the second quarter of 2009 the UK got net financing of $332 billion from three of its Crown dependencies, which had just become offshore tax havens. The island of Jersey had effectively become an extension of the City. The Caymans have become the fifth largest financial centre in the world, with 80,000 companies headquartered there, including three quarters of the world's hedge funds.

Here in Britain the government claims that there is only £20 billion of tax evasion and avoidance but some economists estimate that it could be a £120 billion, and similar tax dodging carries on all around the world. Since Thatcher deregulated the banking system in 1986 and Clinton abolished the bank regulation laws in 1998, the world's been transformed, with wealth being shifted all around the planet so that the super-rich and the giant corporations don't have to pay their share of tax. The consequence of this has been a huge increase in inequality here in Britain, which has doubled in the last forty years so that it is now as bad as it was in 1914. The small square mile of the City of London is now home to 1 per cent of the total world economy. With just 8,000 people living there, that means the wealth is 1 million times the average global rate. Seventy per cent of the world's bond trading, 37 per cent of foreign exchange and 20 per cent of hedge-fund assets are all based in that square mile.

Labour's new leadership under Jeremy Corbyn and John McDonnell would almost certainly be committed to reforming this appalling, unaccountable concentration of power, so we can expect the financial sector to do everything in their power to stop Jeremy getting into Downing Street.

CHAPTER SIXTEEN

London Today

I'm proud of my parents' generation not just because they stood up to and defeated the greatest evil in human history, but in the years after that war they created a world in which everything got better year by year. They forged a wonderful society in which councils were building new homes to rent and the government created economic policies that allowed full employment for thirty years, so that when I left school every child got a job. Crime was low and it was safe to walk on our streets.

The most dramatic change in our lives came when we hit the 1960s, not only with the wave of amazing music but a Labour government prepared to oversee the abolition of hanging, and to legalise homosexuality and the right to abortion. But London was also a city that welcomed people from around the world. We now have probably the most diverse city on the planet but one in which levels of racism and bigotry have been marginalised as people of different races and faiths form relationships and raise their children. The diversity of our city has also been wonderful in creating a range of food options, which I spell out in the chapter on my restaurant-critic days. Thirty-six per cent of Londoners are eating a healthy diet, compared to just 29 per cent nationally, and although binge drinking is a problem for 18 per cent of Brits, in London its only 13 per cent.

A city with 300 languages spoken, fifty communities of over 10,000 each and now half of all the births in our city are by women born outside the UK. In London the average earnings are over £37,000 per year, but that's not a good sign because the inequality is quite stark. In Kensington and Chelsea the average earnings are £151,000 per year, which is a bit better than Newham.

But in some ways London is doing worse than the rest of the country. Thirty-seven per cent of ten-to-eleven-year olds are are overweight or obese. Southwark has the highest rate of teenage pregnancy (one girl out of every thirteen), which is the worst rate in the developed world except for the USA, and a borough like Lambeth sees its children achieving the worst A-level results.

Although I grew up in a generation where virtually everybody could buy their own home or rent a council flat, and even those in private rented homes weren't being ripped off because local councils had control over the landlords, no one can say that about young Londoners today. Whereas my generation could buy their first home in their twenties, today's young Londoners are having to wait until their thirties, and when they do buy their first home a third of them have to leave London because they can no longer afford to buy one in the city they grew up in.

Cocaine use in London is twice the national rate and London has the highest rate of syphilis. Seventy per cent of all the homeless families in England are in London, while Chinese billionaires are spending an average of £6.5 million each buying up homes. As I walk the streets of London I have never seen so many homeless people sleeping on the pavement in my life. One thing that annoys me, given the success of the Congestion Charge back in 2003, is that we are now the second most gridlocked city in Europe after Paris.

A lot of these problems have arisen because since 2010 the governments of Cameron and May have massively slashed their funding for local councils, which are crucial in providing services to our people. By 2020 government funding will have been cut by almost two thirds. My local council of Brent now employs only half the people it did back in 2010.

I feel real anger that today we live in a city where we can't say things are getting better for the younger generations and it's not just because of the savage cuts made by Cameron and May, it's the failure of governments to properly regulate London's financial industry. We now have only 178,000 manufacturing jobs left in our city while the financial sector has surged to 332,000. This all comes down to the legacy of Thatcher and Blair. Ten years on from the global financial crisis that created the greatest recession since the 1930s, the banks still remain free to take risks. The international financial sector remains as powerful as it was before the crash and they have used their influence over politicians to block regulations that would prevent another crash like 2008. In the last few months endless numbers of economists have warned that we are on the verge of another financial crash by 2020.

The biggest scandal is that while the government pumped billions of pounds into propping up the banks, the vast majority of working- and middle-class families have seen the quality of their lives diminish.

We need to recognise what caused the financial crash of 2008. What helped create such a great life for my generation is that we grew up in a world in which the financial sector was properly regulated to avoid institutions taking dangerous risks. Unless we bring similar laws back into play, we will inevitably face crash after crash in the decades ahead. After the 2008 crash there was talk of the banks being broken up and the need for a financial transaction tax but these have just faded away. The simple fact is that the power of the financial sector over politicians is as strong as ever.

In the aftermath of the crash politicians could have made the changes necessary to create the sort of stable economy that was the legacy of Roosevelt and others of the 1930s. But when Barack Obama came to power he did nothing and never had the courage to stand up to the financial sector. Instead the right-wing media and politicians spread worldwide the lie that the financial crash was because governments had spent too much on things like education, the NHS and welfare.

Roosevelt's policies were built on the consensus that something like that should never happen again and he took control of the commanding heights of the economy. But the politicians of my generation, like Tony Blair and Bill Clinton, believed they had to work with the giants of Wall Street and the City of London. We've got to make certain the next generation of political leaders have the courage to stand up, and there are good signs that this is coming. The surge of support for Bernie Sanders in the struggle for the 2016 American Democrat nomination and the biggest rise in Labour's vote in over seventy years following Jeremy Corbyn's election campaign in 2017 show the world is ready to rally behind genuine progressives. Of course the financial establishment will do everything in its power to prevent them coming to office.

While I was researching this book, I came across a speech made by Dennis Healey, Labour's chancellor from 1974 to 1979, when he pointed out that in the twenty years following 1955 firms in Britain only invested two thirds as much as firms in West Germany, half as much as firms in France and just a quarter of what the Japanese achieved. The impact was dramatic: manufacturing employment rose by 11 per cent in France, 31 per cent in Germany and 155 per cent in Japan. In Britain, manufacturing employment fell by 13 per cent.

Clearly, we can never rebuild the old manufacturing jobs that have gone to other nations around the world, but we could move forward in creating the industries that can tackle climate change. Our impact on our planet has been devastating: since 1970 60 per cent of birds, mammals, fish and reptiles have been wiped out and all climate change scientists have told us we have just twelve years left in which to tackle this problem if we are to avoid the collapse of civilisation by the end of the century.

Although 28 per cent of Londoners will die from cancer and 27 per cent from heart attacks and strokes, because of air pollution we have now reached 7 per cent of the population dying as their lungs collapse.

Everyone in my family has died of a heart attack or stroke yet I suspect I'm going to be the first to die of a lung complaint. All my life I have lived in a city where the quality of air has got worse and worse. When I became mayor and introduced the Congestion Charge we saw pollution in the congestion zone cut by 12 per cent. This led me to introduce in early 2008 a London-wide low emission zone in which heavy goods vehicles had to pay to drive into the city. Given that 9,500 Londoners died prematurely every year because of our worsening pollution, I intended to introduce similar charges on all polluting cars following the 2008 mayoral election. But I lost to Boris, who immediately cancelled this policy and in the decade since his election nearly 100,000 have died from air pollution in London.

What is inspiring now is that the current mayor, Sadiq Khan, in April 2019 introduced tough new admission standards for vehicles in central London. The new ultra-low emission zone charge started on 8 April, with diesel cars built before 2015 and almost all pre-2006 petrol cars charged £12.50 a day in addition to the continuation of the Congestion Charge at £11.50 a day.

What is remarkable about Sadiq is that although he faces his next election in 2020, he's honestly committed himself to extending the ultra-low emission zone to cover the whole of London between the North and the South Circular Roads in October 2021. Nearly 4 million Londoners live in this area and will have to pay £12.50 per day to drive. Very few politicians in recent decades would have dared to have made such a commitment in the run-up to the election, but it inspires me to think that Bernie Sanders, Jeremy Corbyn and others around the world who have had the confidence to promise radical change can come to power and give our kids a better life.

I look back at my life over three quarters of a century and see how amazing the scale of change is in our city, but what I didn't realise is how dramatically it was changing before I was born. I was really shocked to read the autobiography of Will Thorne, *My Life's Battles*, which was published in 1925 but relaunched in 1989. Just a poor working-class boy born in 1857, Thorne writes:

I remember my father's death quite well although I was barely seven years-

old at the time ... my first job came when I was only a little over six years of age; it was turning a wheel for a rope and twine spinner at Rob's Rope Walk. I received two shillings and sixpence per week, and worked from six in the morning until six at night. With a half-hour for breakfast and one hour for dinner. On Saturday we worked from six in the morning until one o'clock midday, and when I finished at the Rope Walk I had to go to my uncle, who kept a barber's shop and help him by lathering the customers' faces until about eleven o'clock at night, and then again on Sunday from eight o'clock until two in the afternoon and for this work I was given a shilling a week ... We were so poor at that time that my mother had made an application ... for Poor Law relief and the guardians had granted four loaves and four shillings per week. The bread was about as bad as it could possibly be, and it was my job to collect the relief every Wednesday from the Poor Law office about two miles from my home ... Those were days of hunger for all of us, especially on a Tuesday, when both bread and money had run out. My next job ... was at a brick and tile works ... The place was three miles from our home and each day a six-mile walk was added to the day's work of twelve hours ... I had to handle from four to five hundred bricks a day. As my uncle made the bricks from two moulds I took them and laid them on this hot floor, and generally it was almost impossible to work with my boots and stockings on, so I did not wear any at all. The work was heavy for a lad of my age, each brick weighed about nine pounds, and in the course of a day I carried several tons of clay bricks ... Sometimes we would finish work at five o'clock, but it was generally later ... After being out of work for two or three weeks I got a job in another brick works ... It was a four-mile walk every night and morning and I had to get up at four o'clock every morning to be at work at six ... Here was I, a boy of nine years of age, that should have been in school, getting up in the cold of early morning, leaving home about four thirty, walking four miles to work, and then after a long twelve-hour day, walking back again, a fifteen-hour day by the day I got home, dead tired, barely able to eat my scanty tea and fall into bed.

*

This world described by Will Thorne is just three quarters of a century before I was born but he was inspired to fight for worker's rights and created the National Union of Gas Workers and General Labourers, which went on to become the largest trade union (the General and Municipal Workers' Union) in Britain and ultimately persuaded the government to introduce the eight-hour working day and began to provide social provision for the poorest. Thorne was eventually elected to Parliament for West Ham South in 1906 and remained an MP until he died in 1946. But he and his generation changed Britain every bit as much as we've seen in my lifetime.

People today need to see a world that will change as dramatically in the decades to come as it did during my lifetime and the lifetime of Will Thorne. We have to face the biggest threat to our species in human history; climate change threatens the extinction of most life on this planet over the next century if we can't tackle the problem today.

Every winter in the 1950s London was covered in snow for days or weeks and now it's just a couple of days every decade. Even in the 1960s it was only every few years that we had a nice hot summer; most of the time it was a cool and damp. Last year we had the hottest summer ever recorded in modern times.

Tragically, we have people like Donald Trump who deny any threat from climate change and refuse to take any action, but fortunately Bernie Sanders has announced he is running again for president in 2020. Along with many other candidates, he is now seeking the Democratic nomination, and they are committed to tackling climate change.

Jeremy Corbyn and his shadow chancellor John McDonnell have spelled out how many hundreds of thousands of new jobs can be created as we tackle climate change in Britain.

As we look around the world, all over the place radical new politicians are emerging and proposing the changes we have to make to guarantee a safe future for our children, and it's not only that we've got to cut carbon emissions – we've also got to consume less. The level of wastage that I see as people throw away clothes and food and furniture that they chuck out because they want something new and fashionable is appalling. My post-war generation wasted nothing. What we valued was not spending, but the time we spent with each other and, just as crucial, the drive to create a better world. Not only must we reduce carbon emissions, we have to change the way we live.